Praise for The Serpent and the Staff/ The Mermaid and the Diver: Stalking the Roots of Psychoanalysis

By juxtaposing a great wealth of comparative material drawn from myth and religion, shamanism and alchemy, music and cinema with a series of crystal-clear précis of the seminal insights of the principal theorists of the Freudian and Jungian traditions, the vicissitudes of the healing process, as it unfolds within contemporary Jungian analysis, are vividly born witness to by a master practitioner who is as keenly aware of his own vulnerability within the intersubjective field as he is of his patients'. A cornucopia of insights and amplifications, etymologies and case vignettes, the book also provides, by means of the aesthetic sensibility and poetic acumen of its author, a fresh perspective on the havoc-wrecking, trickster-like role which severe psychopathology may play in challenging the received narratives and normative assumptions in which the psyche in our time finds itself ensconced.

Greg Mogenson, Jungian analyst and author of *Notional Practice: The Speculative Turn in Analytical Psychology*

In this deep and expansive volume, one encounters the breadth of psychoanalytic traditions and its roots in myth, ritual, poetry, music, and alchemy. Experienced Jungian psychoanalyst Ronald Schenk takes us into the experience of psychoanalysis by giving theory and structure their place and at times laying himself bare in the realities of therapeutic work. We feel, through his evocative writing, the writers, the images and the healing rituals. We feel

i

the sincerity and depth of the author. While stalking the roots, he is not afraid of stirring up the mess of psychoanalysis, nor of exposing its muddy matter, and he is certainly not afraid of, as Wilfred Bion described doing psychanalysis, "making the best of a bad job."

Pamela J. Power, Ph.D., Clinical psychologist, Jungian psychoanalyst, author of *Transitions in Jungian Analysis: Essays on Illness, Death and Violence.*

About the Author

Ronald Schenk, CMSW, is a Jungian analyst with a PhD in Phenomenological Psychology and training in psychoanalysis, practicing in Texas as a member of the Inter-Regional Society of Jungian Analysts where he has served in many administrative positions including President and as President of the Council of North American Societies of Jungian Analysis. He has a background in theater and has lived and worked with Navajo Native Americans. He has lectured and published several essays on clinical and cultural subjects and psychological theory and has created a multi-disciplinary presentational mode which includes lecture, song, art, dance and poetry. His previously published books are:

The Soul of Beauty: A Psychological Investigation of Appearance
Dark Night: The Appearance of Death in Everyday Life
The Sunken Quest, the Wasted Fisher, the Pregnant Fish:
Post-Modern Reflections on Depth Psychology
American Soul: A Cultural Narrative

THE SERPENT
AND THE
STAFF

The Mermaid and the Diver

Stalking the Roots
of Psychoanalysis

Ronald Schenk PhD

CHIRON PUBLICATIONS • ASHEVILLE, NORTH CAROLINA

www.ChironPublications.com

Interior and cover design by Danijela Mijailovic
Printed primarily in the United States of America.

Front cover image "Tree Roots and Trunks" by Vincent van Gogh, Public domain, via Wikimedia Commons.

ISBN 978-1-68503-511-2 paperback
ISBN 978-1-68503-512-9 hardcover
ISBN 978-1-68503-515-0 electronic
ISBN 978-1-68503-513-6 limited edition paperback
ISBN 978-1-68503-514-3 limited edition hardcover

Library of Congress Cataloging-in-Publication Data Pending

To
    My patients
        Who were my supervisors
        And to
            Harvey, Don, John and Jeff

"whatever you have to say,
leave the roots on, let them
dangle

And the dirt

Just to make clear
where they come from"

Charles Olson – "These Days"

Table of Contents

Acknowledgements

This book is meant as a companion to my previous publication by Chiron, *The Sunken Quest, the Wasted Fisher, the Pregnant Fish: Postmodern Reflections on Depth Psychology* (2001). I am grateful to Murray Stein, Publisher Emeritus, and to Jennifer Fitzgerald, Editor, for her considerable help in navigating the complexities of the publishing process.

I would like to thank the editors of Spring Journal for inviting me to write on alchemy and also acknowledge my debt to the ideas of James Hillman for what has become the first two chapters of this book. Chapter Three on rhetoric and therapy came out of a rewarding class with Robert Kugelmann in the Psychology Department of the University of Dallas. I am grateful to James Hollis for his years of friendship and sustenance, and his involvement with 1) the C. G. Jung Educational Center of Houston and the opportunity to present the chapters on Ritual and Myth, and 2) the Jung Society of Washington D. C. and the opportunity to contribute to its program the case study of Chapter Nine. In this regard I owe gratitude toward my patient, "Dee" as co-subject for our enriching work together. My thanks to Nancy Furlotti for inviting me to join her and her colleagues in casting another glance into the depths offered by dreams. Professor Nathan Link generously signed off on my meditation on Bach and psychoanalysis, and Arlene Landau graciously invited me to share my thoughts on "Undine" for Psychological Perspectives. My good friends and colleagues, Nancy Dougherty and Jacqueline West, have been immensely supportive over the years, and I am very appreciative of what I have learned through their invitation to review their study of psychopathology. The work of Nathan Schwartz Salant is an invaluable cutting-edge contribution to any thinking regarding severe psychopathology and its treatment and was an inspiration for the last chapter on the overriding interaction of order/disorder in our work. This book has been decades in groaning self-deliverance, and I am obliged to the determined, persevering tolerance of my wife, Charlotte, for enduring my "eternal return" to its emergence.

Introduction

The term "depth psychology" was coined by Eugene Bleuler at the time of the emergence of psychoanalysis—the turn into the 20th century—as a way of designating the theory and practice of the study of the psyche that focused upon the workings of the unconscious. The word "depth" speaks of what lies beneath, invisible, in the dark, in the realm of the underworld, and as James Hillman points out, pertaining to death, all as a fundamental matter of soul.[1] In other words, depth psychology, through the psychoanalytic attitude of mind, looks to in-sights from what is un-seen as a mode of *understanding* soul (*psyche*) in its most authentic form and place, depth as the work, where the action is.

The purpose of this book is to explore the underworld of depth psychology, to reveal and make clear the murkiness and interacting multiplicities of its foundations—even as the field struggles to maintain its integrity in the face of cultural emphasis on expediency, and cultural challenges such as that presented in relationship generated and contained through technology. It does so while finding itself in an internal and external environmental *ethos* which it attempts to undermine: overdetermined rationality, cause-effect thinking, literalizing orientation, humanistic values and personalizing positioning, engrained ego identification, and heroic striving. This subversive gesture extends to bear upon conventional "knowing" via the objectification of parts at the expense of a wider, less readily comprehensible, imagistic, contextual whole of experience. In this light it is an attempt to move the psychoanalytic approach out of its traditional foundation in the dynamics of 19th century physics and beyond the outdated, abstract, conceptual frameworks of its tradition toward an ontological emphasis on experience in the moment as revealed through reverie and awakening. In other words, the current attempt is to extract from its own primal ooze an orientation related to the core of the psychoanalytic project, catching the paradoxical meaning of the co-experienced space in its unfathomable depths and unreachable breadth by means of imaginative curiosity.

The words in the title refer to figures and actions that present themselves in the psychoanalytic imaginative space. The serpent is the chthonic, autonomous, instinctive, larger-than-life aspect of healing, at the same time both toxic and curative; the staff is the Apollonian, man-made, prescription or container. Divers represent the psyche's agency for investigating underneath the surface, while the mermaid reflects alluring, primeval energies thriving below while lurking above, each in desire of the other. "Stalking" as a verb indicates the means by which analyst and patient move cautiously, stealthily, sneaking up on that which is either threatening or receding by following traces and tracks that lead through stickers and snarls, around potholes and bottomless pits into an underlying swampland of primary sources. Paradoxically, "to stalk" also means the opposite, "to walk haughtily with high, stiff steps," which one must do at times in passionate cadence with psychological emergence. As a noun, "stalk" connects what is below the surface with what is above, so that the title suggests creating a connection between the underworld and the light above. "Roots" bespeak foundational, fundament, basic, origin, source, ancestral world acting as anchor, yet stretching outward, expanding domain, supporting in their passivity. As a verb, "to root" signifies digging out, determinant, sexual intercourse, and vehement encouragement, penetrating in their aggression. Roots undermine dualism in that they both nurture and choke, and while they are usually thought of as tending downward, the alchemical World Tree is rooted in the sky, an expression of the dictum "as above, so below."

This work is meant as an analysis of psychoanalysis itself, and therefore the overlapping, interrelated dynamics of the analytic enterprise is reflected in the inter-active, emergent, rootlike inter-connection between the chapters and their contents. Trotting out the suspects: the first two chapters investigate the notion of "Beginnings" as an archetypal, ubiquitous, ever-present place or condition with a life of its own regardless of what occurs subsequently. Using the alchemical notion of *prima materia* in its many manifestations, we look to the importance of achieving an image of what beginning form is at hand in order to activate the proper procedures. The wide variety of beginning conditions that alchemy differentiates gives the analyst a multiplicity of ideas to stimulate imagination and curiosity as to what lies below and beyond in the work.

One archetypal beginning is the "Word," the idea that rhetoric (language, words, talk,) itself is a subjectivity that has a primary healing function. Analysis is fundamentally the "talking cure," and some schools of analysis see the unconscious as organized through language. Words are considered not as tools, rather, themselves as subjectivities that "speak the speaker," affording a glimpse into unconscious life. Ritual, in its many forms of evoking memory, is a fundamental aspect of all healing. Psychoanalysis becomes a place of rituals in a forgetful culture enamored of newness, and analysis itself emerges as an eventful reenactment of the primary rite of "crossing over" in return to origins—developmentally, archetypally and existentially.

Out of ritual emerges myth, bringing in aspects of "story" as essential to a core element of the autonomous nature of healing. Myth informs analysis in the sense that the individual psyche is living out a personal narrative reflecting a universal image, and that the healing process itself has its own myth—or story. Ritual and myth come together in the experience of the nightly dream, and gnostic myth acts as guide to consciousness entering dreamlife.

Ensuing chapters illustrate the interactive nature of the psyche starting with the idea that identity itself is a fluid, kaleidoscopic, ever-emergent enterprise, which informs psychoanalysis in the inter-subjective nature of the therapeutic field. Counter to the notion that selfhood is a matter of interior subjective consciousness and unconsciousness, identity formation is introduced as a matter of "mirroring," taking in the contextual gaze of an "other." The analytic relationship can then be seen as a phenomenon of kaleidoscopic interactions on a primarily unconscious plane. The foundational dynamic of the psychoanalytic event is the circulating flow of energies and appearance of agents in necessary relationship to what is offered as other in the co-constituted analytic field. A case acts as illustration, tracing the meandering threads weaving the relationship in various colors and vectors while giving evidence that ultimately all consciousness occurs through a psychologized body as its own author.

The final two chapters ask the question, "What's happening, man?" while looking into the essence of psychopathology from the underlying standpoint of *pathos*, etymologically "event," and revealing the primal movement of the psyche toward disorder. Two primary ways of seeing psychopathology, developmental and archetypal, are considered as complementary interacting visions. The book concludes in an unsettling fashion, taking the position that pathology and disorder are ultimately inevitable and necessary aspects of psyche, finally focusing on the borderline condition as paradigmatic of psychological life itself.

In conclusion, therapists and psychoanalysts hourly deal with the darkest, most difficult and mysterious aspects of the human psyche. It is hoped that this book may be helpful by providing a deeper and wider context for this, the perplexing, paradoxical "work" (*opus*) of the psychoanalytic enterprise which can only be entered through a plunge. Jung wrote: ". . . the true physician does not stand outside his work but is always in the thick of it."[2]

Endnotes

[1] Hillman J., "Depth" in *The Dream and the Underworld*, pp. 24-27.
[2] Jung, C. G. (1968) *Psychology and Alchemy* CW 12, Trans. R. F. D. Hull. Princeton: Princeton University Press. 6.

Chapter One

Alchemical Awakening: The Initial Mess[1]

"To begin at the beginning"
        -Dylan Thomas, "Under Milkwood"

"In my beginning is my end"
        -T. S. Eliot, "East Coker" (I)

"In the buginning is the woid"
        -James Joyce, *Finnegan's Wake II*

I receive a phone message from a prospective client. His voice is soft and deep, but something about it seems overly mature. His speech has an air of formality that feels somewhat forced, like something is being held in confinement. He mentions his referral source, and I feel gratified that this individual has thought of me. I am feeling drawn in. The caller gives his phone number, but adds that he will not be available to answer the phone before 10:00 a.m. I ponder as to the reason— late sleeper? not working? Is there some kind of self-indulgence here? But then, I am an early morning person myself, and maybe my puritanical inclinations are intruding, my *senex* evoked by his *puer*, my pathology already part of the dialogue. When I call the number after the specified time, the man answers. His voice is soft, now seemingly effeminate, but again in a somewhat forced way. His language is formal, careful, protective, but he seems grateful for my ready response, knowledgeable about the location of my office and eager to get started. My trickster aroused, perhaps testing or maybe even provoking him, I give a time convenient for me but before his previous 10:00 a.m. boundary. I am a little surprised when he takes it. I am then taken aback when he mentions that his mother will be paying for the session and asks if he should bring the check himself or have her pay directly. I had his age pegged as anywhere from late 30's to early 50's, and now his mother is paying! I wonder about what I am getting into as we end the conversation. Does he have a weird dependency or some kind of latent or passive aggression? A beginning has taken place.

I have agreed to write a paper on alchemy, an ancient enterprise of interacting theory and practice which provides highly evocative metaphors for use in the often perplexing realm of psychoanalysis. Where should I start? With an explanation and history of alchemy? An explication of the connection between alchemy and psychology? Or the place of alchemy in Jung's thought? Predictably and as always, alchemy itself has an answer. Alchemy designates the beginning as the *prima materia* and elaborates on it. I think a quick explication will be easy. I have notes from classes and workshops, books, Xeroxed papers, tapes of lectures, etc. Once into it, there will be a flow, a snap, no problem.

The writing doesn't happen. Time goes by, and the deadline approaches. I find ways of distracting myself. Other concerns take on a larger importance, greater priority. I shuffle through my material, but I get pulled into going deeper into what was to be only the initial subject. I feel sluggish; the material is boring, and there is too much of it. I wrack my brain for examples. They don't come. Sliding around from one false start to the next, I remember a Laurel and Hardy sketch. The two are in a car packed to the gills, but with each attempt to start, accompanied by endless rounds of "good-byes," something goes wrong—the engine needs to be cranked, a tire bursts, something is forgotten, something doesn't work, somebody wants something, etc. The entire movie is the attempt to get started. For alchemy, the *prima materia* is a world unto itself. I will have to limit my subject to just this—the beginning.

The Bible commences with the words, "In the beginning," and speaks of God, and God's initial creations. The Greek poet, Hesiod, introduces his poem, "Theogony," calling upon the Muses, sources of inspiration, and Homer sets the Iliad into motion with anger, and the Odyssey with the "many ways" of Odysseus. There is always a context or condition in the origination of any enterprise. It is dark, only chaos exists, there is no wind, the battle is at a standoff. Something there is that continually draws us back to this beginning situation. We create a category of "creation myths," but all myths are originary. T. S. Eliot said that each new poem rewrites the tradition. Every situation: an analytic session, a relationship, a class, the founding of a nation, the beginning of an organization, the germination of an idea—everything has an initial place, most often not the stated mission, to which the project continually returns.

As a way of understanding how the beginning condition works in psychoanalysis, we turn to alchemy, which in every aspect of its theory/practice serves as one of our best metaphorical models for the psychoanalytic enterprise in all of its depths.

"Through the first gate,
Into our first world, shall we follow
The deceptions of the thrush? Into our first world?"
                              - T. S. Eliot, "Burnt Norton" (I)[2]

Alchemy – an Introduction

Alchemists dealt with concrete substances, matter, and they thought of material as having a singular essence, subjectivity, or soul. Alchemist Morenius wrote:

"Know that (the work) has but one (root), and but one matter and one substance of which and with which alone it is done, nor is anything added to it or subtracted from it."[3]

The substance itself, like the dis-eased object state within the psychoanalytic patient, suffers and rejoices, is mortified and energized. Further, each substance has a certain effect on each of the other substances attracting, extracting, repelling, dissolving, coagulating, concealing, revealing. In addition, the matter and the alchemist were interchangeable. According to Morenius: "Truly this matter is that created by God, which is firmly captive with you yourself, inseparable from you, wherever you be, and any creature of God deprived of it will die."[4]

The dynamics of alchemy are enacted through matrixes of interacting subjectivities—alchemist and material, one material with another. There is no clean subject-object split, rather a constant shifting emphasis between two entities as either subject or object. Alchemy gives a truly interpersonal perspective in that it views everything as both material, as in: "Visit the interior of the earth; through purification thou wilt find the hidden stone,"[5] and subjective, as in: "This matter is extracted from you, for you are its mine."[6] The substance is personalized in alchemy, just as the many internal presences in one human "personality" can be thought of in terms of "substances." The "work" (*opus*) is both a working upon, and a being worked upon. The alchemist, like the analyst, is changed while changing, cooked while cooking. The world becomes an infinite chain of signifiers between subject and object, worker and material, with no final resting place. Alchemy serves as a model for the dynamics of the psychoanalytic event taking place between patient and analyst.

Paracelsus defines alchemy as "the set purpose, intention, and subtle endeavor to transmute the kind of the metals from one to another."[7] As Paracelsus' definition tells us, alchemy's work is one of transformation. Since alchemy sees the world as ensouled, it is already in flux, in process. Matter is always already renovating under the sway of Nature's purpose, and the alchemist's work is to help Nature change the world. The *Rosarium*, an alchemical treatise on the mystical marriage:

> "You should employ venerable Nature, because from her and through her and in her is our art born and in naught else: and so our magisterium is the work of Nature and not of the worker."[8]

The first part of the work prepares the material so that it will take its initial form, the *prima materia*, from which proper alteration can occur. The "first" step is actually a two-fold process—recognize the initial appearance of the matter and prepare it by bringing it to its initial form.

The term, *prima materia*, originates with Aristotle for whom it meant "something that isn't there." Paradox: a matter that isn't a matter! Right from the start, alchemy teaches us to see with a non-literalizing, double vision. There is something, but also something else. The end is always something previous, so we are already beginners at the end point. Aristotle is referring to a potentiality which is not actualized because it has not taken on a particular form that will be imposed from without. For Plato, the potential form is that which lies latent within or beyond. Whether imposed or emergent, *prima materia* is a matter of inherent potential.

"And the bird called, in response to
The unheard music hidden in the shrubbery,
And the unseen eyebeam crossed . . ."
-T. S. Eliot, "Burnt Norton" (I)

The idea of a ubiquitous source or original state is itself a universal metaphor—"beginning" as archetypal. The Greeks of antiquity thought that the entire universe started from one substance, the original stuff, a permanent unity, an underlying unchangeable identity the nature of which depended upon the diagnostician, as it does in psychoanalysis. Greek philosopher Anaximander saw it as an undifferentiated mass, the "boundless," and emphasized the latent conflict of the opposites, especially between hot and cold, wet and dry. For Anaximenes, it was "air," "mist," and "fog"—for Heraclitus, "fire." Where the Greeks did agree, was that in this source was the condition for transformation.

Likewise, the alchemists theorized that to bring about change, one had to first create the proper starting condition. "All error in the art arises because men do not begin with the proper substance."[9] As with the Greek philosophers, there were conflicting opinions among alchemists regarding the exact nature of the beginning. Some thought it had to do with mercury, others lead, water, fire, etc. Paracelsus considered "death" to be the start and end of all processes.

"From wrong to wrong the exasperated spirit
Proceeds, unless restored by that refining fire
Where you must move in measure, like a dancer."
- T. S. Eliot, "Little Gidding" (II)

The *prima materia* was concrete material and also an attitude, a way of being, a philosophy, a world. Greek general and generalist Olympiodoros elaborates on the sense of totality that lies in the notion of *prima materia* when he refers to "our lead" as distinct from common lead. Common lead was traditionally used to cover coffins and was black to begin with. By contrast, alchemical lead starts out a different color than black and must be darkened to achieve the proper beginning condition. Olympiodoros refers to alchemist and mystic, Zosimos's, notion of the egg as an image of the cosmos containing the four elements:

"They call lead the egg—I mean the egg of the four elements—that is what Zosimos says, and by that he really always means lead. If they explain its shape (*eidos*), they really in secret allude to the whole thing, because as Maria says, the four elements are one."[10]

Lead as egg is a thing and a way of thinking, a metal and a mind, an ore and a world.

"At the still point of the turning world. Neither flesh nor fleshless;
Neither from nor towards; at the still point, there the dance is,
But neither arrest nor movement..."
T.S. Eliot, "Burnt Norton" (I)

From the standpoint of alchemy, material always implies a dynamic. Nothing is more inspired than matter, nothing more material than spirit. Something appears in the beginning, but something is also not there, and whatever is there, is also not there, and whatever is not there is there. Change comes about as a process of the visible, or lower form, coming into alignment with the invisible, or higher form, and the opus or work of alchemy is to help this change along.

Paracelsus and the *Materia Prima as Principia Ultima*

Paracelsus, the great alchemist of the Renaissance is the most explicit of the alchemists in laying out the complex qualities of the Beginning or First Condition relative to the work of alchemy, which we are using as a template for the project of psychoanalysis as a process in the evolution of soul. In Paracelsus we are seeing metaphorical change within the patient from the original psychologically dis-eased condition to one of renewed form in alignment with a more genuine personality. For Paracelsus, the work of alchemy is to help Nature's, or God's, project of changing impurities (psychopathology) into essences, (more authentic being,) materia prima to materia ultima. Paradoxically, the first matter and the ultimate matter are, at the core, one and the same.

> "The first principle with God was the ultimate matter
> which He Himself made to be the primal, just as a fruit
> which produces another fruit .."[11]

The primary matter is like a seed, which if treated with appropriate care becomes the plant or metal or creature it essentially is.

> "The first matter of things, that is to say, the matter of
> principiating principles is begotten by Nature, without
> the assistance of any other seed; in other words, nature
> receives the matter from the elements, whence it
> subsequently brings forth the seed."[12]

"Nature begets a mineral in the bowels of the earth,"[13] and it, as "first essence," becomes potential life, a fetus hidden in the womb. In working with the matter, it is imperative to determine its actual content ...

> "It ought to be known what the primal matter is
> according to its essence. For the primal matter has in
> it such virtues that it will not allow the body, which
> is born of it, to go into consumption, but abundantly
> affords whatever is necessary for the supply of every

requirement."[14]

The ultimate matter is a goal or state, alike in essence, but different in form from the prima mater.

> "Whatever is to pass into its ultimate matter must become something different from what its origin was . . . In the beginning, it must be remarked, concerning the Primal Matter, that it puts forth its predestination, to which it is foreordained, entire, and from its first origin to its final end well-defined and exemplified."[15]

This change is a renewal, an original form regenerated.

> "For as the seed gives of itself the entire herb, with renewal of all its forces and consumption of the old essence, so that the former substance, nature, and essence have no further operation . . . *we are born from one seed like something growing in the field according to its growing nature* (italics mine)."[16]

Paracelsus thinks of the process of change as "digestion," hence accompanied by a sense of torture and death. Another alchemist, Bonus of Ferrara, also sees alchemical transformation in terms of digestion and describes it as: ". . . the gradual development of that which is conceived by gentle outward heat,"[17] i.e., the evolution of a metal comes out of the digestive conjoining of one with another. Digestion implies a kind of death, and for Paracelsus, the entire process is "the transposition of the metals from one death to another."[18] "Destruction perfects that which is good."[19] A seed in the ground must "purify" and "dissolve" to emerge eventually as that plant, metal, creature, or form that it is meant to be in its visibility.

> "The good is least good whilst it is thus concealed. The concealment must be removed so that the good may be able freely to appear in its own brightness . . . Each one of the visible metals is a concealment of the other six metals."[20]

Change is a matter of fluctuating revelation and concealment resulting in an ultimate appearance or emergence or extraction of a substance, "clear in its *esse*."[21]

Paracelsus finally fits alchemy into an image of the cosmos of stones and stars. The stones, or seeds of the earth, reflect the stars as informing spirits. The three-fold evolution of the seed or metal through the opus of alchemy is a matter of an evolving vision of the intentionality of imagination, which "kindles the vegetative facility like fire kindles wood."[22] It starts in its gross appearance, is reduced to its place of origin, and then emerges in alignment with the stars as world soul.

We can see in these images a correlation with the psycho-analytic endeavor as one of an initial diseased state of mind in the patient becoming something more genuine through a process of gentle heating or digesting or reverie until a new form in alignment with authentic character emerges.

Psychoanalysis

Patients come into psychoanalysis and are depressed, or anxious, or angry, or can't function, or harbor labile emotionality, or are afraid of intimacy, or of abandonment, or don't know what the matter is, or don't know who they are, or where they are headed, or hold themselves back, or self-destruct in various ways. These are all states of soul with corresponding visibilities as symptoms—boring job, distanced relationship, can't get up in the morning, teary eyes, bent body, etc. Visibilities are in the presenting problem, but also in the initial encounter, not just the first phone call or the first meeting, but in every session. What is the face saying today? And the body? Or the first words? Or the analyst's condition in relation to any or all of these indicators? Once into the session, a clinician will be interested in one or more of a variety of beginning situation forms. Curiosity, or imagination, is the driving force for the analyst, who wants to know when the presenting problem started, and what was going on at that time. How has this appeared before? What is being recreated and relived? What originating circumstances and figures are knocking on the door? In the wings more details are awaiting their entrance—significant others of the moment or the lack thereof? Family of origin? The couple's first meeting? How did you get here? What has the journey been like? What brings you in now? This initial stuff is important because it represents the past's inevitable play on the present. Ultimately, the question in the back of the analyst's mind might be, what about this beginning situation touches me, and how am I going to fit into the story?

And last, the rending pain of reenactment
Of all that you have done, and been; the shame
Of motives late revealed, and the awareness
Of things ill done and done to others' harm
Which once you took for exercise of virtue.
- T. S. Eliot, "Little Gidding" (II)

Alchemy helps psychology to see that the apparent starting condition, be it "diagnosis," "presenting problem," or "initial impressions," is a matter of substance. Through the eyes of alchemy, the presenting problem is matter appearing in an unfinished form, the ore—unrefined, the metal—imperfect, its soul in pain, ugliness, or disquiet. Alchemy considers these external situations to have an internal correlative; nature is always doubled, both within and without at the same time. So, the alchemical clinician sees the beginning situation with a metaphorical eye. Something is concretely there, a concealed seed of authentic self, but something else is also happening that prevents its emergence. Alchemy presents the psychotherapist with a multitude of complex images with which to imagine this dynamic. At the same time, alchemy is able to see in everyday life a wide variety of experiences that point to a beginning condition, and it is to these phenomena that we will turn in the next chapter.

Out of Air emerges Matter.

Endnotes

[1] A version of this chapter initially appeared in *Spring 74 Alchemy* as "The Alchemical Attitude of the Analytic Mind: An Introductory Primer on *Prima Materia* for Initial Beginners at the Start." I am indebted to James Hillman's University of Dallas class on alchemy as its inspiration.

[2] All quotations from T. S. Eliot are taken from T. S. Eliot, *The Complete Poems and Plays 1909-1950*.

[3] Stavenhagen, L. ed., A *Testament of Alchemy*, p. 13.

[4] Stavenhagen, p. 27.

[5] Basilius Valentinus in Titus Burckhardt, *Alchemy: Science of the Cosmos, Science of the Soul*, p. 101.

[6] Morenius in Stavenhagen, p. 27.

[7] Waite, A. ed., *The Hermetic and Alchemical Writings of Aureolus Philippus Theophrastus Bombast of Hohenheim, called Paracelsus the Great*, Vol. I, p. 16.

[8] Jung, C. G., "*Rosarium Philosophorum*," *The Practice of Psychotherapy*, CW 16, p. 212.

[9] Jung, C. G., p. 212.

[10] von Franz, M. L., *Alchemy: An Introduction to the Symbolism and Psychology*, p. 82.

[11] Waite, p. 91.

[12] Waite, p. 293.

[13] Waite, p. 36.

[14] Waite, p. 40.

[15] Waite, 39.

[16] Waite, 39.

[17] Bonus, Petrus of Ferrara, *The New Pearl of Great Price*, p. 24.

[18] Waite p. 9.

[19] Waite p. 4.

[20] Waite p. 4.

[21] Waite p. 9.

[22] Waite p. 7.

Chapter Two

Hands in the Mess:
Prima Materia in Psychoanalysis

"Our only health is the disease."
- T.S. Eliot, "East Coker" (IV)

1) *Prima materia* is chaotic, a *massa confusa*, a confused mass, or just a mess. It seems out of control, irrational—an autonomous life that wants to devour anything and everything. "It's eating me alive." An alchemical image of Cerberus, the monster dog that guarded the underworld, depicts a three-headed monster, each head ready to devour a being while other figures are clutched in the paws, and entangled in the tail.

A college-age male comes in for therapy. The son of parents who divorced when he was three and the object of each of their narcissistic needs, he has been depressed and anxious all his life. His emotions came to a head during the past year when he was involved in an accident in which he was a passenger in a car struck by a drunken driver, who pulled out of line and ran a red light killing a good friend who was driving. The young man is ridden with guilt but also harbors a secret sympathy with the uncontrolled aggression of the offending driver. Here, the confused mess is both a mixture of feelings, and the tragic event of recklessness and wreck (which occurred outside of analyst's office, hence....)

2) It is ubiquitous—everywhere and anywhere. Wherever I go, there I am. Work, vacation, marriage, affairs, friends, family—the same things come up in each situation.

"This Matter lies before the eyes of all; everybody sees it, touches it, loves it, but knows it not. It is glorious and vile, precious and of small account, and is found everywhere . . . To be brief, our Matter has as many names as there are things in the world; that is why the foolish know it not."[1]

The Arabian alchemist Ab'l Quasim al-Iraqi describes *prima materia* as:

" . . found in a mountain which contains a measureless quantity of uncreated things. In this mountain is every kind of knowledge that can be found in this world. There is no knowledge, understanding, dream, thought, skill, interpretation, consideration, wisdom, philosophy, geometry, statecraft, power, courage, distinction, satisfaction, patience, discipline, beauty, inventiveness, travel, orthodoxy, leadership, exactitude, growth, command, authority, richness, dignity, counsel or business, which is not contained therein. But also, there is no hatred, malevolence, deceit, infidelity, illusion, tyranny, oppression, corruption, ignorance, stupidity, lowness, despotism or excess, and no song, game, flute or lyre, or marriage, no jest, no arm, no war, neither blood nor homicide, which is not contained therein."[2]

A woman worked on her mother problem for years focusing on a wide spectrum of circumstances in which the effects of her mother were at work. The mother had indicated to her as a child in a variety of ways that she was unwanted. Finally, the patient sensed an improvement in herself as she worked to integrate feelings which had been repressed her entire life. She then had a dream in which she was in a boat crossing a body of water to an unknown area, and when she got to her destination, there to greet her was . . . her mother.

3) It is inert in nature and therefore resistant to change. The patient says, "No matter what I do, I still feel the same way," or

"All I've got today is what I've been talking about all along." The prima materia is indestructible, stone-like, cold and immutable. It gives the soul an experience of being held prisoner, reflecting spirit's imprisonment in matter, the incurable old king, or the mind's imprisonment in spirit.

> *A dreamer enters a Zen Buddhist monastery, walks through various rooms where people are in meditation and winds his way to the extreme back room where he finds the American head of the monastery sitting in a hot sweat box, head covered in sweat, face contorted in pain, body invisibly suffering in heat.*

Energy is tied up in conflict, leaving a feeling of being stuck, unable to move, void of possibility, suffocated, helpless and hopeless, unchangeable. In therapy, the patient thinks an initial insight means "It's fixed!" But, to his consternation, months and then years pass, and the condition persists. The resistance and its analysis, or "working through," becomes everything. In alchemy inertia is represented in names "lead," "our lead," "lead of the air," "Saturn," "Saturn's child." Maria Prophetessa considered lead to be the basis of the work, but Olympiodoros referred to the oracle Peasios, who warned that lead was so "bedeviled and shameless" that those who want to learn about it fall into madness.[3]

> *A man in his late 40's with a soft, passive demeanor, comes into analysis complaining of a persistent ambivalence in his life. He has been married for over twenty-five years to an entitled, paranoid woman with whom he has little relationship except to take care of her considerable financial needs, and he spends a great deal of time, money and energy with a mistress and her children. He is a lawyer, dealing in bankruptcy, but finds himself cleaning up the messes of people he doesn't like, while his secret passion lies in writing.*
>
> *As a child, his father absented the family while the patient served the needs of a histrionic mother and played fantasy war games by himself. During the course of analysis, the patient reported a recurring dream as a child in which*

a wolf persistently was trying to get into the house. The analyst thought back to the first session, when he found himself feeling alternatively bored and unruly as if to growl and mistakenly ended the session 10 minutes early. The analysis ground on for months and years during which time the patient's digestive system was insistently, rumblingly problematic. At one point, the patient was forced to have eye surgery to prevent blindness.

"Dust in the air suspended
Marks the place where a story ended.
Dust inbreathed was a house
The wall, the wainscot and the mouse,
The death of hope and despair,
This is the death of air."

- T. S. Eliot, "Little Gidding" (II)

4) It repeats itself; perseverating, appearing over and over, again and again. It's *deja vu* all over again one more time. The patient says, "I sound like an old record!" The "black pitch," like the tar baby, keeps sticking. "I can't get away from it." "Haven't we been here before?" "It won't let go." "I feel compelled in my compulsion." "I can't get this strange thought or silly song out of my head." There is a fascination about it. "I feel like I am enchanted." It is irresistible, exquisitely seductive, "the whore of Babylon." ... perpetual regurgitation, over and over creating, destroying, being created, and being destroyed.

A man in his fifties comes into analysis anxious, depressed, angry, and questioning the meaning of his life. He is highly judgmental of himself and bears low self-esteem punctuated with erectile problems. An insurance salesman, he finds himself unappreciated by his employer as has been the case throughout his career. He feels confused, can't find meaning in his life, and wants an answer to his life's suffering in an overarching philosophical system. As a boy, he was equally influenced

24

by a schizophrenic mother, who consistently gave him mixed messages, and an abusive father, who undermined his attempts at self-expression before committing suicide. After several years of analysis, in which he struggles through several jobs, finally finding one that seems to fit, and after achieving a sense of identity in relation to his wife, child and grandchildren, the patient develops prostate cancer and comes to his session anxious, depressed, angry and questioning the meaning of his life.

"Where is the end of them, the fishermen sailing
Into the wind's tail, where the fog cowers?
We cannot think of a time that is oceanless
Or of an ocean not littered with wastage
Or of a future that is not liable
 Like the past, to have no destination.

We have to think of them as forever bailing."
- T. S. Eliot, "The Dry Salvages" (II)

5) It is *increatum*, unformed being, green, unripe, or prematurely pure, innocent, naive, rosy-cheeked, white-washed, without fault, or syrupy sweet, inviting violation.

A woman in her mid-thirties, a mother of two children and herself a housewife, finds little identity outside of her prescribed role, a "girl in a box." As a girl, she suffered a great deal of emotional isolation while taking on the responsibilities associated with alcoholic parents. She reports a recurring nightmare of being chased by a dark figure.

It is emptiness, a void, vacuum, or abyss—the black hole at the pit of the stomach of individuals with a lack in early attachment experience and an abundance of abandonment, identified with associated compensatory glowing imagery without substance. "No problem!" "Cool breeze, man!" "I didn't realize . . ." "Who . .

me?" "Butter," "the milk of the virgin," or "virgin's milk," it is overly rich, fatty, creamy, hokey.

A man in his early thirties of artistic temperament and vocation, who was raised in an abusive and chronically chaotic environment in which he was forced to take on a great deal of responsibility, finds himself having problems creating boundaries in a personal and professional life that is in perpetual turmoil. He smiles a lot, has a great deal of charm, and starts each session talking about how great things are in his life.

"Dry the pool, dry concrete, brown edged,
And the pool was filled with water out of sunlight,"
 - T. S. Eliot, "Burnt Norton" (I)

6) It is called "turb," a turbulence or storm, which sweeps through, creating havoc in the established order-affect, psychic energy, moods, tears, rage, fear, the "undisciplined squads of emotion" (T. S. Eliot, "East Coker," V). Wallace Stevens wrote that out of nothing, comes major weather. It is bi-polar, either afire with manic activity or stultified with humiditas radicalis, "moisture," "oily water," the "fatty water." It is the labile affect, or mood swing, or perpetual weeping. It is "the sodden, moist, fat, and muddy earth of Adam . . . from which this large world, we ourselves, and our powerful stone were created."[4] On the other hand, it is the "red sulfur," a kind of drivenness to "do something," get on with it, let's buy something or just "get out of here." It is "lead of the air," a flurry of airy activity with a depressive foundation, the eagle tied to the toad, the god to the peasant.

A man in his mid-thirties has been working at a feverish pitch in the corporate world all his career, but he feels himself stuck of late, his life void of relationship, direction, or identity. His mother is a new age artist and his father, an overly disciplined academic researcher. After spending a prolonged vacation practicing yoga and Tantric sex in India, he decides to move there to start a new business.

It is the "Muladara," or "salamander"—the instinct which provides the limits of efforts for socialization.

A promiscuous fifteen-year-old girl from an impoverished chaotic family says of sex, "Ah gots to have it!"

"On a summer midnight, you can hear the music
Of the weak pipe and the little drum
And see them dancing around the bonfire
The association of man and woman
In daunsinge, signifying matrimonie"
                    - T. S. Eliot, "East Coker" (I)

It is—*ira*, irate, rage—the cultural shadow of a violent society, where the value of Anger as guide is lost, and it is seen as only destructive. It is the "fire in the water," the anger underneath the tears, the energy underneath the boredom, the "hidden fire" of secret desire waiting for an adequate container in the world.

A man who has been seething with rage for a year over a broken relationship and now quieting, dreams that he has come across a series of foundry ovens filled with ashes from fires long gone out. In another dream, he sticks his hands into the ashes of an abandoned fire and feels what turns out to be a skull.

"Water and fire shall rot
The marred foundations we forgot,
Of sanctuary and choir.
This is the death of water and fire."
                    - T. S. Eliot, "Little Gidding" (II)

7) It is "other," alien, unwelcome, weird, odd, unrelated to, reviled, repugnant, denigrated, dis'd, disliked, disowned, discounted, disregarded, "wowed," in disrepair, or disguised. Its names are the "orphan," "accursed of God," "dung," and *vili figura*, the vile figure. "The substance that we first take in hand is mineral . . . It is of great inward virtue, though it is vile to the sight. . . . It is of

venomous nature."[5] This is the ruined woman, the broken man, the identified patient carrying the family sickness, the outcast or scapegoat in a group, as well as the part of the individual personality that is most shameful or carries the most guilt, the worst part of the most repugnant, the "menstruum of the whore."

A woman in her early forties comes to analysis because her only daughter, a teenager, has suffered from an eating disorder. The mother would like to "work on her stuff." She divorced the father of her daughter eleven years previously, and in the intervening years the daughter has had a great deal of contact with the father. As the feelings of the mother start to reveal themselves, it becomes clear that she suffers from underlying guilt at not being able to "heal" her former husband's depression. She has been afraid that her daughter's illness is connected to the daughter's emotional caretaking of the former husband. Further, the patient comes to realize that she also carries guilt associated with her inability as a girl to "heal" a schizophrenic older brother for her own mother.

"There is only the fight to recover what has been lost
And found and lost again and again . . ."
                              - T. S. Eliot, "East Coker" (V)

The taste is bitter, like vinegar, the salt of sea water, *amaritudo* or the salt of tears, the "rhubarb water." A patient says, "I stood alone in the parking lot and cried, shedding scales of pain and loneliness." The alchemists bear witness to the bitterness but see in it eventual wisdom. Michael Maier writes: "There is in our chemistry a certain noble substance, in the beginning whereof is wretchedness with vinegar, but in its ending, joy with gladness."[6] George Ripley writes: "Each thing in its first matter is corrupt and bitter. The bitterness is a tincturing poison."[7] "In the bitterness that is in its (the wingless bird's) throat the coloring will be found."[8] Mylius: "Our stone is endowed with the strongest spirit, bitter and brazen."[9] This is the venom-dripping pout, resentment, or the look of "silent sulking scorn" as one man ascribed to his wife. "O nature and of this wondrous thing, which transforms the body into spirit! . . . When it is found alone it conquers all things, and is an excellent, harsh and bitter acid, which transmutes gold into pure spirit."[10]

It is a wounding remark, sharp, biting, a dart thrown out during conversation, a joke cutting too close to the bone. It has a bad smell, "the stench of the graves," connected to the underworld, putrefaction, corruption, decay, decadence. Words erupt from the ass, *flatus voci . . .*

A young girl in play therapy starts each session by blessing the playroom with farts in each of the four directions, making herself complete by allowing her lower voice to be heard from all perspectives.

It is the "slime of the small world"— the little things, irritations, petty grievances, and annoyances. In the myth of Inanna's descent, it is dirt under the fingernails, which gets the whole process going when it becomes stagnant in the underworld.

"Garlic and sapphires in the mud."
- T.S Eliot, "Burnt Norton" (I)

8) *Prima materia* is associated with pain and called Lucifer, Hades or "affliction of the soul," which is applied to the substance and the worker at once, a dark tone of *nigredo*—dying, torture, devouring, suffocating, contorting, sinking, being skinned alive, shaven bare, stripped to the bone, Nessus' burning shirt of fire.

"Who then devised the torment? Love.
Love is the unfamiliar Name
Behind the hands that wove
The intolerable shirt of flame
Which human power cannot remove."
-T. S. Eliot, "Little Gidding" (IV)

A successful businessman in his 50's, very thin and gaunt, a cyclist and spin instructor in his leisure, comes into analysis disgusted with his adopted adolescent son's gluttony and sloth. During the course of analysis, he develops esophageal cancer for which he receives painful treatment, and it recurs twice. He gradually becomes aware of his own needs, which have been squelched in childhood when his family coped with a handicapped sibling. The work becomes a movement toward the realization that he could, in fact, relax, have his cake and eat it too.

9) It carries paradox, the experience of it and the opposite at the same time. It is "Mercurius," the "hermaphrodite," he of "two natures," who "runs round the earth and enjoys equally the company of the good and the wicked."

"I am the poison-dripping dragon, who is everywhere and can be cheaply had. That upon which I rest, and that which rests upon me, will be found within me by those who pursue their investigations in accordance with the rules of the Art. My water and fire destroy and put together; from my body you may the extract the green lion and the red. . . . I bestow on you powers of the male and the female, and also those of heaven and of earth . . . father and mother, young and old, very strong and very weak, death and resurrection, visible and invisible, hard and soft; I descend into the earth and ascend to the heavens, I am the highest and the lowest, the lightest and the heaviest, I am dark and often the order of nature is reversed in me light; I come forth from heaven and earth; I am known and yet do not exist at all . . ."[11]

"The fiery and perfect Mercurius" refers to synchronistic happenings—spontaneous combustions, out of the blue—"I don't know what got into me."

It is "Luna," moon mystery, moonshine, difficult to hold, constantly evaporating, vapor, "twilight zone," uncertainty, ambiguity, flux, fantasy, dead ancestors, half-life, limbo, things occult. The moon is the place where soul and spirit separate according to Plutarch, and under the moon arise suicidal thoughts, the spirit yearning for freedom, as well as images of rebirth.

It is "Word" as seed from heaven, "In the beginning was the Word," and all the mercurial qualities of language—Freud's slips of the tongue, Jung's association experiments, puns, metaphors and metonymies, words as images, words as worlds with histories, associations, etc. "I'm blocking!" "I can't think of the word." "It's right on the tip of my tongue." "It just popped out of my mouth."

A woman with progressive political sensibilities, yet feeling a lack of agency in her life, dreams of sleeping with Donald "Trump," a reviled figure whose last name expresses an action she finds repulsive and who she associates with a power-hungry family narrative by which she was victimized. Analytic understanding clarified that her psyche was using a dream figure metaphorically referring to the type of power she had been keeping at bay in herself and was now beginning to connect with.

"And so each venture
Is a new beginning, a raid on the inarticulate
With shabby equipment always deteriorating
In the general mess of imprecision of feeling."
                              -T. S. Eliot, "East Coker" (V)

10) It is the ground, fundament, parent—the "sea," aqua permanence, itself the container holding all forms, or the "tree" that grows on the surface of the world—sea branching out into all entities, or the "earth," which nurtures all beings, or the "red earth," which receives all elements.

"The parched eviscerate soil
Gapes at the vanity of toil,
    Laughs without mirth.
        This is the death of earth."
                              -T. S. Eliot, "Little Gidding" (II)

A male dreamer is toiling, shirtless, dripping of sweat, taking down outhouses in the hot midday sun, shoveling dirt like mad into privy holes full of shit and piss ready

*to be incorporated back into the earth, and folding up
the lumber of the outhouses to be moved on to another
location.*

It is the "Mother" or the "Father," not literal people back in all those Midwestern towns or in the Bronx, but the feelings and principles to which one always comes back—the Unum, Adamica, "Adam," First Man, original form, ur, "where it all began," "the root of itself."

*A lawyer in his fifties comes to analysis complaining of
the after-effects of successful prostate surgery. His sexual
libido which has been prominent throughout his adult life
has diminished. At the same time, he has come to realize
that he is quite dissatisfied with his work with a large firm
cleaning up the legal ecological messes of corporations.
The main focus of his analysis comes to be dealing with
the anxiety in leaving the safe confines of his work both
at the office and at home, care-taking his depressed wife
and schizophrenic daughter, both derivatives of his job as
a boy with a volatile and irrationally rageful mother and
a shopkeeping father. His secret project is to build his own
eco-business, taking care of "Mother Earth" in a unique
and innovative way based on incentives for profit.*

It is the body as carrier of turbulence, psychosomatic indicators—rashes, inflammations, infections, cancers, ulcers, infections, endometrioses, allergies, colds, headaches, autoimmune diseases, syndromes chronic fatigue and Epstein-Barr, all potentially held by patient and by analyst.

"Yet the enchainment of past and future
Woven in the weakness of the changing body,
Protects mankind from heaven and damnation
Which flesh cannot endure."
- T. S. Eliot, "Burnt Norton" (II)

11) It has the quality of the divine, the "golden head," without beginning or ending, in need of "no second," having the nature

of God, or "The One," Unica Res, "Monad," pure subject, "the infinite"—"It's all one, man!" "That from which things arise is the invisible and immovable God."[12] It is the identification with grand questions—all black or all white—Where are we going? Who am I? What is this all about?

A young man dreams that he is on the edge of a cliff in the middle of a hot day watching two giant bears far below, one black and one white, fighting a ferocious battle to the death. All of a sudden, he feels something at his feet. A brown chipmunk is nibbling at his toes. Something small, grounded, and difficult to catch in his psyche is calling him away from the ineffable big stuff.

12) It is already the goal, the fruit of the work, the Philosophers Stone, autonomous and eternal. What is "despised and rejected" is also the saving grace, the "Redeemer." What starts in the stables, among the animals, becomes a world savior. I may dislike my anger or be afraid of intimacy or be burdened by guilt and shame or be confused about my identity or lack of direction, yet within these emotions lies exactly what will allow for change. That which is concealed wants to be revealed and integrated. The "gold" or "eternal water" or "joy with gladness" that marks the *prima materia*, is the process of continually recognizing and incorporating what is already there.

"... both a new world
And the old made explicit, understood
In the completion of its partial ecstasy,
The resolution of its partial horror."
                                        -T. S. Eliot, "Burnt Norton" (II)

A middle-aged businessman comes into analysis feeling "something dark underneath pushing upward like a force" and becomes tearful as he speaks of what he will call the "Mother of the Monster" after a figure in the Old English epic, "Beowulf." After many years of analysis and life experience—loss of job, divorce, death of a close family member—he finally comes to experience the derivative of an inner rage that has been kept in check by admonitions of parental figures from an early age. A dream during this process depicts the patient alone at a campfire near a cliff wall, out of which emerge ancestral figures that have been depicted as petroglyphs on the wall. They dance around the fire, and he joins them. He ultimately finds himself at board meetings able to cut through bullshit to achieve an appropriate orientation to the different levels of process. Likewise, in his personal life, he finds himself able to be direct with others. At the same time, his fire for "business as usual" in work and "running the mill" of false attempts at relationship diminishes. He pulls back from business and social life, invests his time with family and devotes his energy and money to charitable causes.

> "Not the intense moment
> Isolated, with no before and after,
> But a lifetime burning in every moment
> And not the lifetime of one man only
> But of old stones that cannot be deciphered."
> -T. S. Eliot, "East Coker" (V)

Alchemy gives clinicians an image-based attitude of mind with which to approach the work of psychoanalysis from within a perspective of a different order than the ruling rational mind. The contents of psychological life can be thought of as substances. The substances are worlds of being with their own qualities which include the analyst/therapist, transference and countertransference, always already in co-creation of a third realm. The work of analysis is a work upon the substance, but also the work of the substance upon the therapist/analyst and patient. The substance presents itself as a place to start from, a home of sorts, but also a dwelling of disaffection holding the rupture between meaning and experience. Each session becomes another new beginning, another delving into the inarticulate invisible, a new striving for a current revelation at hand. The work becomes a process of opening so that a surprise may occur and be received, shucking the old shell so that what one is and has been is seen through a different perspective. A fresh set of expectations and assumptions, hopes and loves emerge, largely for the wrong things again but this time closer to the mark while at the same time creating a different set of problems. With the new alignment comes a consciousness nearer the goal of being with the moment and a new faith—one in imagination as a mode of living . . . out . . . the same old stuff.

The primary material is ultimately the "other," anything unexpected, "not me," a surprise waiting to appear. It can occur at any time in any session, and in analysis as in daily life, the emergence of an "other" brings up pitfalls of the beginning condition. One tendency is for the analyst to make it something that suits one's own needs, rather than letting it appear in its raw form. I want to contain my own anxiety by imposing control or grasping the situation prematurely rather than letting it work on me. I want to take immediate action, to literalize, get on top of it, rather than to imagine the metaphorical image within which I am now dwelling. When I have the "other" fixed, my own pathos recedes. I become comfortable in my control and don't have to feel threatened by the uncertainty, chaos, confusion, darkness, ugliness, messiness or terror of the beginning which alchemy sees as essential.

Another problematic first tendency is for the clinician to shrink back from the pathos of the beginning by getting caught up in a variety of analytic modalities. Over emphasizing the diagnostic or typological label, asking for dreams, referring to a clinician of a different gender or orientation, consigning the patient as untreatable—all serve as a means of diversion. More explicitly, directive interventions such as prescribing a mode of feeling or action or technique only serve the defensive purposes of the therapist. Ultimately, any direction of consciousness that diverts her from an awareness of intimate connection with the patient, sets the ensuing interaction off on the wrong path. As the old saying goes, "A sow's ear is a sow's ear." A sculptor is automatically Platonic, looking at the initial mass of wood or marble or clay, not from the standpoint of intentional form, but through a sensibility for the autonomous life of the particular substance. She knows that the final form lies latent in the subject, and to allow it its autonomous presence, she has to avoid imposing an image which is comforting to her. The Zen master, Shunryu Suzuki, spent years teaching a simple idea, "In the beginner's mind there are many possibilities; in the expert's mind there are few."[13]

To end on a note of sobriety, inevitably there are times when the seed doesn't take, the resistance of soul too great. Our original patient from the opening of chapter One, the man who had called for an appointment, turned out to be a college dropout with a history of alcohol and drug abuse associated with parental divorce and a highly disruptive maternal presence. He was determined to give himself a new start, get into therapy, get a job, get back in school, etc. He attended a few sessions, revealing a highly ambiguous, primitive tie to a dominating mother against whom he was struggling to separate. He did manage to get a job and shift some of his dependence to his father, but he didn't last long in analysis, dropping out of the therapeutic container unable as it was to hold his terrible mercury.

Out of the Mess emerges the Word.

Endnotes

[1] Edinger, Edward, *Hermetic Museum,* in The *Anatomy of the Psyche,* p. 11.

[2] Burckhardt, Titus, *Alchemy: Science of the Cosmos, Science of the Soul,* p. 100.

[3] Jung, C. G., *Mysterium Coniunctionis,* CW 14, p. 351.

[4] Burckhardt, Titus, "*Theatrum sapientiae aeternae*" by Heinrich Kunrath, p. 104.

[5] Edinger, Anatomy *of the Psyche: Alchemical Symbolism in Psychotherapy,* p. 12.

[6] Jung, *Psychology and Alchemy,* CW 12, p. 273.

[7] Jung, CW 14, p. 19.

[8] *Ibid,* p. 192.

[9] *Ibid,* p. 192.

[10] *Ibid,* p. 192, p. 245.

[11] Jung, *Alchemical Studies,* CW 13, p. 218.

[12] Jung, CW 12, p. 323.

[13] Suzuki, S., *Zen Mind, Beginners Mind,* p. 21.

Chapter Three

Rhetoric and Therapy

"She (Anna O.) aptly described this procedure (hypnosis), speaking seriously, as a 'talking cure,' while she referred to it jokingly as 'chimney sweeping.'"
-Joseph Breuer and Sigmund Freud, *Studies on Hysteria*

"Do you not know that words are healers of the sick temper?"

-Aeschylus, *Prometheus Bound*

Logotherapy of Ancient Greece

The ancient Greek world gives an image of how, across cultures and throughout the ages, language works to heal. In the ancient Greek world, *physis*, was considered as nature—that which is born, germinates and grows, and ultimately takes form through fertility. It is that "regularity with which a visible outward appearance reveals the latent existence of a particular quality."[1] The notion of disease was originally one in which physis (of the subject or patient) was acted upon through loss of soul, penetration of object or possession by an evil force. This evolved into one in which the "nature" (*physis*) of the individual was seen as contaminated in the form of punishment for a transgression, crime of an ancestor, or possession by a god or *daimon*. Gorgias states in his Eulogy of Helen, "Charms (*epoidai*) inspired by the word produce pleasure and banish pain; in fact the power of the charm, intimately frequenting the fancy of the soul seduces her,

39

persuades her, transforms her by means of a sort of sorcery."[2] He compares the words to the action of a medicament, because the word (*logos*) modifies *physis*.

Asklepios, son of Apollo and god of healing, learned "charming" words from the Centaur Chiron. He would speak to the patient, utilizing the healing power of words both in form and content. Speech itself serves as healer as well as the healing signifiers contained in the words. According to Galen, Asklepios would even assign his patients the task of composing odes and skits to correct the proportion of emotion in their soul. The treatment of disease was thus achieved through *logos*, the "word," in the form of song (*oide*), often addressed to the god who caused the disease. In a larger sense, "logotherapy" existed in the form of prayer and persuasive speech, the *epode*, charm or conjuration, used predominately to compel nature. "The dear sons of Autolykos were busy to tend him, / and understandingly they bound up the wound of stately / godlike Odysseus, and *singing incantations over it* (italics mine) / stayed the black blood, and . . . / healing him well . . . sent him / speedily back rejoicing to his beloved country . . ."[3]

Here the Greek verb *deo* means to bind by literal tying, as well as the act of enchanting, the two being seen as interconnected. Enchantment of the disease is one of two forms of the healing power of words given by Apollo, god of healing, whose symbol was the staff. The *paean* was another name for song or prayer used in rites to "enchant" the disease or wound as Glaukos does in his prayer to Apollo.

". . . listen /
to a man in pain, as now this pain has descended upon me. / For see, I have this strong wound on me, and my arm on both sides / is driven with sharp pains about, my blood is not able to dry and stop running, my shoulder is aching beneath it. /
. . . my lord, make well this strong wound; / and put the pains to sleep, give me strength, so that I may call out / to my companions, the Lykians, and stir them to fight

on, . . . So he spoke in prayer, and Phoibos Apollo heard him. / At once he made the pains stop and dried away from the hard wound / the dark running of blood and put strength into his spirit."[4]

A second form of therapeutic usage of language is manifested in the oracular function of words. The prophets not only foretold the future but conferred benefits both public and private; the seer, *mantis*, and the physician, *iatros*, are the same. Socrates in Plato's "Phaedrus" attests to the benefits of madness associated with prophecy.

". . . in reality, the greatest blessings come by way of madness, indeed of madness that is heaven-sent. It was when they were mad that the prophetess at Delphi and the priestesses at Dodona achieved so much for which both states and individuals in Greece are thankful . . . madness was accounted no shame nor disgrace by the men of old . . .

. . . when grievous maladies and afflictions have beset certain families by reason of some ancient sin, madness has appeared among them, and breaking out into prophecy has secured relief by finding the means thereto, namely by recourse to prayer and worship, and in consequence thereof rites and means of purification were established, and the sufferer was brought out of danger, alike for the present and for the future. Thus did madness secure, for him that was maddened aright and possessed, deliverance from his troubles."[5]

Ndembu Linguistic Healing

Anthropologist Victor Turner did his field work with the Ndembu tribe of Zambia in Central Africa focusing on curative ritual and in particular the related semantic structure of the symbolism.[6] He found that the Ndembu chose their healing substances from trees whose names reflect medicinal powers. A certain species of tree whose roots are exposed is called *wuvumbu*, derived from the word *ku-vumbuka*, meaning to be unearthed, thereby having power to bring disease "to the surface." The *chikwata* tree has strong thorns, which "catch" one passing by, and its extract likewise is thought to pierce the disease with its strength. The name of the *musong' asong'a* tree is etymologically derived from the term for "to bear fruit," *ku-song'a*, hence the effectiveness of its powers to enhance childbearing, *ku-songa anyana*. The *muhotuhotu* tree is used to combat conditions involving falling, as its name is associated with the word *ku-hotomoka* meaning "to fall suddenly" hence acting as a form of inoculation. The *mutunda* tree, whose name is derived from the word, *ku-tunda* meaning "to be higher than those around," carries powers of growth and health. The mupapala tree holds properties for treating epileptoid conditions based on its name being derived from the word *kupapang'ila* meaning "to wander about in confusion." An initiatory ritual for girls involves lying under the *mudyi* tree while participants dance around it. The extract of the tree is a milky substance, such that the tree itself enhances the movement into motherhood.

All of these sources of healing based on semantic symbolism parallel in their own way, the symbolic techniques in psychoanalysis of teasing out the complex, gaining conscious "power" by verbally "working through," exercising imaginative reformulation of the complex based on its structural context, "inoculation" via reliving of traumatic experience, expansion of ego strength via identification with internal ideal objects, analytically bringing about clarity of focus to avoid confusion, and the gaining of emotional maturity to move into a more evolved psychological realm.

Navajo Healing Through Language

For the Navajo, the most powerful element in the universe is air and its motion. The control of this action, through speech, in turn gives gods and humans power. One of their major divinities is named "Talking God," and the world was created through the actions of the gods sitting in a hut and chanting or "singing" the world into being by giving words to thoughts and speech to those words. Anthropologist Gary Witherspoon wrote:

> *In the Navajo view of the world, language is not a mirror of reality; reality is a mirror of language* (author's italics) . . . The language of Navajo ritual . . . determines how (things) will be . . . It commands, compels, organizes transforms, and restores. It disperses evil, reverses disorder, neutralizes pain, overcomes fear, eliminates illness, relieves anxiety, and restores order health, and well-being.[7]

The Navajo world exists according to a certain order called *hozho*. Words create this order and repair breaks in that creation. Improper connection with *hozho* causes pathology in humans. Pathology is caused by influences from evil gods, other humans in the form of curses of witches or "skin-walkers," improper contact with animals, exposure to natural phenomena, improper connection with a ceremony, contact with the dead—all of which may have come about historically in the life of the individual. Healing is brought about by the restoration of alignment with order through rituals which in part entail the power of words through chants or "songs." These chants are recited word perfectly, some lasting over lengthy stretches of time, a practice which reflects the inherent order of the universe. The "compulsion by exactness of word"[8] indicates the transformational power held by the proper use of words to bring about healing. Words themselves, rightly ordered into form, are a divinity with a personality of its own. According to a Navajo singer: "Prayer is not like you and me; it is like a Holy Person; it has a personality five times that of ours."[9]

In Navajo healing ceremonies, the patient is brought into identification with the power of beneficent gods through language—chants, sung by a medicine man or "singer,"[10] which take the patient back into mythical time. Chants also bring the patient into identification with the destructive power of the gods of which the patient is then ritually purged, again through chants. This part of the ceremony is particularly delicate because if anything is not performed exactly correctly, the patient could be left injured psychologically. Finally, the patient may be brought into identification with a deity that then transforms evil by travelling to the land of the dead to battle the god who caused the disease and thereby recover the soul of the patient. In effect, Navajo language performs the function of the shaman, doing what the shaman himself does in his healing practice.

These uses of language correspond to psychotherapy. The identification with a beneficent god through chanting would correspond in psychotherapy to the incorporation of an idealized object or an ego ideal in the person of the therapist. The identification with "evil" through chants may be seen when a patient becomes identified with a split off part of him or herself that has been repressed such as fear or anger. These qualities are then "seen" in the therapist, who holds the emotion until the patient can take it back or integrate it. Finally, the transformation of "evil" is the equivalent in psychotherapy of the "working through" process, the going over and over of problematic experience until the self-healing power of the patient has been activated and gains enough psychological strength to confront his or her inner demons and integrate them into the personality.

The myth of the "Stricken Twins" (to be examined in detail in Chapter Five,) tells of the origin of a healing practice among the Navajo, and specifically the role of language in the healing ceremonies. Two stricken brothers (the sons of Talking God!)— one blind, the other lame, journey from one set of gods to the next seeking cure. Each attempt ends in failure for lack of the proper items to give to the gods resulting in further travail until at one point the gods take pity on them. The boys are subjected to the intense heat of a sweat lodge and admonished not to utter a word, or the spell of the healing power will be broken. They persevere through the ordeal and find themselves cured, only to break their promise of silence and exclaim their joy. Their infirmities return, and they set off down the trail in renewed sorrow. This time, however, they give vocal lament to their despair at their plight. The gods hear their sounds and, pleased with what they hear, call the boys back, requesting of them where they learned such beautiful sounds. The boys can only confess they were sounding out their grief at their condition. Again, the gods decide to help the boys only this time giving them tasks as to how to procure the items needed to give over to the gods for a cure to take place. The boys successfully complete the tasks, are cured by the gods, and bring back to their people the sounds they made as songs to be used in healing ceremonies.

In both the story and the ceremonies, we can see similarities with psychotherapy through the working of language. Just as the boys are "discovered" by the gods and discover themselves spontaneously through their songs, reflecting the creation of the world through chants, so the psychotherapy patient comes to recognize aspects of self as mirrored in words. The Navajo see healing qualities in the linguistic connection of that which is transcendent (unconscious), the gods, with that which is mortal (conscious). The western notion of the unconscious is indicated in the words of a Navajo singer: ". . . the most important thing I learned from my grandfathers was that there is a part of the mind that we don't really know about and that it is that part that is most important in whether we become sick or remain well."[11]

In psychotherapy, the linguistic connection of unconsciousness, the unknown realm, with consciousness, that which is known, is therapeutic. Factors seen as causative—historical, malign influences of important others, as well as derivatives of underlying affects that are resisted, are brought into conscious knowing through the patient's words. Likewise, just as the Navajo patient is placed into a profound relationship with the past both personally and mythically through connection with gods via the singer's songs and chants, the very words of the psychotherapy patient bring about a return to personal and mythic past. Eventually, concealed aspects of the self are revealed, a kind of re-membering of parts of the psyche in its totality.

The myth of the Stricken Twins indicates language as the core of psychotherapy.[12] In the sweat hut, the boys were forbidden to speak, and that is what would bring about the cure.

Maintaining silence, not speaking, holds the power of language within the interior of the psyche, just as silence in the analytical hour serves to build a heat of emotional intensity. The capacity for silence entails the ability to hold, and one of the primary tasks of psychotherapy is to create a space for reflection and revery through containment of affect as opposed to discharge through action. This is paradoxical because the action of verbalizing is one of the foremost means that psychotherapy, the talking cure, uses to get to the concealed aspects of the personality.

Breaking the container by exclaiming their joy led to another expulsion and loss for the twins. Their expression became groans, the groans became words, and the words became songs. This event was a "return to origins" in that it replicated the formation of the Navajo world by the original deities who thought, then formulated thoughts into words, then spoke the words into the world's being. The unutterable sound that came forth from the boys was that of groans, expressions which came from an unknown part of themselves. (The archetypal nature of this event is seen in the Christian myth when Paul writes in his letters to the Romans, "The whole creation groaneth and travaileth in pain together until now . . . even we groan within ourselves . . . the Spirit itself maketh intercession for us with groanings which cannot be uttered" (Romans 8:18-27).) A new depth of expression had been achieved and when these groans turned to songs (the first blues?) the sound was beautiful and desired by the gods. It was these songs that became the songs and chants of an actual Navajo healing ceremony, the sound of suffering, formulated into language, bringing about cure, and it is this use of language, mythically dictated, that serves as an enlightening mirroring reflection of the linguistic foundation of Western psychotherapy.

The myth indicates how foundational linguistic metaphors of psychotherapy have an underlying concrete form in archetypal healing narratives. The hero twins are born of a virgin mother and divine father, wounded, and make their burdened way along a meandering path, all images which parallel the story of Christianity's central healer, Jesus. The elliptical pattern of the boys' movement from one group of gods to another reflects the circuitous pattern of the repetitions of the "working through" process in psychotherapy where over and over the patient recounts similar responses to life circumstances. What we might call the "journey" of self-discovery is imaged by Jung as a "snakelike" path toward authenticity of self. "It is a longissima via, not straight but snakelike . . . a path whose labyrinthine twists and turns are not lacking in terrors."[13] Jung is saying that through a journey of self-exploration, the patient finds what had been "inaccessible," and through ancient Greek, native African, and Navajo healing, we are able to see this journey as one carried by language.

Out of the Word emerges the Act . . .

Endnotes

[1] Entralgo, P., *The Therapy of the Word in Classical Antiquity*, p. 16.

[2] *Ibid*, p. 88.

[3] Homer, *The Odyssey of Homer*, p. 294, p. XIX, p. l. pp. 455-461.

[4] Homer, *The Iliad of Homer*, p. 344, p. XVI, p. l, pp. 514-529.

[5] Plato, *The Collected Dialogues of Plato*, p. 491, p. 2, p. 244 a, e.

[6] Turner, V., *The Ritual Process*.

[7] Witherspoon, G., *Language and Art in the Navajo Universe*, p. 34.

[8] Reichard, G., *Navaho Religion: A Study of Symbolism*, p. 288.

[9] Gill, S., "Prayer As Person: The Performative Force in Navajo Prayer Acts," *History of Religions*, p. 143, 17:2.

[10] The more accurate translation of the term "medicine man" in Navajo is "singer."

[11] Bergman, R., "A School for Medicine Men," *American Journal of Psychiatry*, p. 664, 130:6.

[12] Kugler, P., *The Alchemy of Discourse: Image, Sound and Psyche*.

[13] Jung, C. G., *Psychology and Alchemy*, CW 12, p. 6.

Chapter Four

Ritual As Healer: Return to Origins

I am about to have a session with a patient. I go about my consulting room ordering the chairs, couch, pillows and Kleenex. I look over my notes from the last session, check the accounting of fees and get any receipts ready. I check the room temperature and make any adjustment in the fans, vents and thermostat that is necessary. I go down the stairs and into the waiting area to meet my patient. I notice the look on his/her face and give a short greeting. I process up the stairs following the patient. We make our entrances into the office and take our places: I, in my chair, the patient either on the couch or in a chair. I wait for the patient to start.

The patient begins the encounter in any of a number of ways: silence, sighs, words, with eye contact or distancing, with hard, readily forthcoming preparation or soft, tentative "feeling out" the situation. All of these expressions are the continuing of an immediate narrative that began in the waiting room and even beforehand—on the road to my office, in bed on a sleepless night, in the bath, on the job or at dinner, from the last session and on into the past. As the narrative unfolds, it can build to passionate climaxes and drop into quietude, generate affective turbulence or distillate into calm, ascend to heights or descend into depths.

The patient's narrative generates a complementary internal narrative of response in me, the analyst, of darkness and light, sweetness and sour, highs and lows, unruliness and calm. Additionally, the characters in the narrative are evoked and interchanged between the two parties as the atmosphere generated by the two interweaving narratives takes its form, embracing the two. The event is a kind of spontaneous performance involving preparation, cleansing, supporting psychic structures in place, evoking painful objects, transforming alignments, and eliciting self-healing modalities. At the end of the prescribed time, the patient does or does not pay the fee depending on previously agreed upon arrangement for payment and departs with the trust that no matter how chaotic life becomes, the regularly scheduled analytic hours with the analyst will be there for her to use in any way she chooses.

Ritual

These events can be seen as enactments of ritual in healing, analogous to those practiced throughout the span of ages and cross-culturally. In the encounter of psychoanalysis between doctor and patient, as in all healing relationships, lies the embodiment of many rituals. From the "procession" to the office, to the regime of meeting at the same time and same place at regular intervals, to the unique prone body position of the patient on the couch or seated position in the chair, to the various events within the therapeutic relationship, to the closure of the session, psychoanalysis is imbued with ritual, and ritual itself can be seen as part of the healing process. To illustrate this thesis, we shall explore the healing practices of ancient Greece, ritualistic healing in various native cultures, going into more detail with the Navajo of North America, and finally, the Western precursors to psychotherapy.

The word "rite" means "to do" or "action," and is associated with numbers, the action being conducted in a formal way. Its roots lie in the Vedic sense of "visible order," and its Latin meaning suggests "proven way." It is also associated with "religion" which signifies "bending back" or "careful consideration," "in alignment with stars." Ritual is primordial energy enacted, a return to sacred beginnings, a re-doing of what the gods have done, a re-creation and entering of sacred time to bring about alignment with the totality of being. Ritual, then, is action in service to formulating a larger, more encompassing "reality" by bringing about relationship with that which has gone on in the past and at the same time, that which is intended in the future. The beginning serves as a holding place for the end, the end as the re-emergence of the beginning in a new constellation. The ritual process, conducted in a liminal realm outside of time and space, is "therapy"—*therapeutes* meaning "to wait upon," "to attend to," "care for," or "serve"—in that it brings a new alignment within the subject and a new relationship with collective order. The psychoanalytic event can be seen as a ritual process of "serving" (*therapeutese*) the "soul" (*psyche*).

If healers of the psyche serve the soul, they ask, what is it the soul wants? What works or what is at work in the "care of the soul?" We will see that answers to this question are at once universal, healing modes as archetypal, and culture bound. What works in the healing practice of any one culture toward serving the soul in distress comes out of the values of that culture. Western psychoanalysis comes out of a cultural condition, in which subjective "life" is internal and the forces to be dealt with are concealed in internalized structures we call the "unconscious." Native cultures are known to consider the human soul to be inextricably bound to external factors alive in the world, such as various aspects of nature, as well as spirits and demons. What is common to both is to bring about a condition of harmony with "larger than" life forces either external or internal through ritual.

Healing Ritual in Ancient Greece[1]

As we have seen, for the ancient Greeks, there was *physis*, nature, matter in its essence or the natural flow of life symbolized in the serpent, and *nomos*, "custom," "convention," or "law," what man does with nature symbolized in the staff. One goal of *nomos*, in this case, ritual-building relative to "psychotherapy" or "care of the soul," is that of *pronoia* or "foresight," creating a new vision or way of seeing. This "revisioning" could only come about with a "return to origins," an encounter with the source. The Greeks considered sickness as being caused by a god and considered the source of healing to be the god that brought the sickness about. "He who wounds, also heals," as the Greek adage goes, just as in psychoanalysis regression into the complex is the first step to ultimate integration. Therapy in the Greek sense was a homeopathic enterprise of revisiting the source of the disease or creating a condition in which the source could be addressed or connected with, as childhood is revisited in contemporary psychoanalysis. This event could only occur in a sacred space or *temenos*, "place where divinity appears." The *temenos* was sacred in that it was a liminal space, one in which mortals with points of view, expectations, assumptions and actions typical for the culture in daily life, would encounter that which was "beyond" the everyday, in this case, the divine. The most famous of these was Epidaurus, the temple of Asklepios, god of healing.

The healing rites of Epidaurus began with the procession to the temple of patient and family. In certain instances, the procession is depicted as a labyrinthine journey through the underworld, in others, a form of gathering of energy participated in by the gods associated with healing. A symbolic payment was given over to the god—a sacrificial rooster, pig, or goat or models of the afflicted body part. Here there is something of reciprocal exchange in healing—the god needs something the wounded possesses, just as the wounded needs something from the god. The patient was then purified through cleansing and led into the *abaton*, ("place not to be entered unbidden") the inner-most chamber where he would lie on a mat or couch to sleep, a form of incubation (*incubare*, "to lie down upon," "to sleep in sacred precinct"). The patient went to sleep to induce a dream, a call to the god that caused the disease, sleep symbolically indicating a giving up of willful control. If the rite proceeded successfully, the god would appear in the dream in one of many forms—animal, boy, old man or as the god itself—and address the dreamer symbolically with words, touch, gesture or even lick or bite. Upon awakening, the patient was led to a seat where he/she was asked to remember the events of the night before.

The rites of Epidaurus present a model for healing that can be seen in rituals of many cultures and in psychoanalysis. The procession to the temple can be imagined as a kind of pilgrimage in preparation to enter a different reality, akin to the walk of patient and doctor into the therapy room or "chamber." This space, like the *abaton*, is a liminal space where doctor and patient meet, not as social beings as in ordinary life, but as psychological "figures" in a story intending to relate in a way that is "beyond" the everyday in order to explore that space which is not normally accessible to daily contact.

The "giving over" to healing powers through sacrificial presentation is accomplished in psychoanalysis through the technique of free association, giving over ego control to a flow of consciousness, (as well as the giving over of the fee.) Universally, healing cannot occur until something is given up to the higher powers, "I give that you may be with me." Ritual cleansing or purifying conducted in the healing of many cultures is, again, a means of preparation, a baptism, in which painful residues of conscious life are subjected to a dissolution. In psychoanalysis, this might be seen in the initial moments of settling in and reflection that the patient undergoes. The process of lying down to sleep took the ancient Greek patient literally into a different reality akin to the state of reverie, the giving up of rational consciousness and intentionality that is induced by the vulnerability of the horizontal position on the couch or relaxed position in the chair.

The crucial "return to origins" through confrontation with gods or spirits thought to have caused the "disease" takes many forms and in psychoanalysis is the confrontation through narrative memory with unconscious contents of traumatic events and unrealized potentials—images ridden with guilt, shame and despair or desperately yearned for, fantasies of imagined happenings, forbidden thoughts and feelings, and crucially, the exploration of intangible presences like friends and enemies— old and new, bosses and parents, family and unknown strangers. Often the facing of the repressed content takes place in dreams through confrontation with an animal or feared figure chasing the dreamer or trying to get into the dreamer's quarters just as the dreams of ancient patients evoke divinities.

A different kind of ritual, which had healing aspects of initiation and a renewed sense of well-being, occurred at the temple of Eleusis, "place of happy arrival." Here the annual rites of initiation were held in honor of the goddess of fertility, Demeter, and her daughter, Persephone. Eleusis was the actual place where, according to myth, Demeter, grieving in search of her daughter, sat at a well and laughed at the antics of the female trickster Baubo. In the ritual actions or *dromenon*, Persephone emerges from the underworld and presents Demeter with an ear of corn. A child appears in a flash of light with a pronunciation of new life. The provision of well-being for the initiates occurred in the learning of a secret or the revelation of "mystery" (*mystei*, "those with closed eyes," *myein*, closed, *mythos*, "that which is not told").

Again, there is a procession, this one of several miles, consisting of initiates and attendants, ritual cleansing in the sea or in a Salt Lake, and the sacrifice of animals. Also present in the procession are baskets of offerings, containers, each holding a certain seed, and a mask of Dionysus, the "Great Loosener," god of theater. At the temple, the initiates are led in the dark through a labyrinthine passageway, imitating the wanderings of Demeter to the place of epiphany. Here, healing is revealed as a form if initiation, (from Latin *in-itia*, "going into,") an entrance into darkness, back to origins, down into roots. Ritual as stepping in the footsteps of the gods to achieve a more complete being.

Preparatory rituals were performed—passing an object back and forth between containers, the presentation of a winnowing fan and vessels containing seeds and a sacred marriage between a boy and a priestess. Finally, the climactic epiphany occurred—a flash of light, a form of *agnonorisis*, or symbolic recognition, and a voice declaring, "Brimo begets Brimos," the annunciation of new life in the form of an ear of corn seeds and the emergence of the daughter as the birth of a child. Now, Demeter has ended her wanderings, her grief has lifted, she has made peace with the gods and now reveals her mysteries to humans through enabling a new vision of life.

The psychological underpinnings of the rites of Eleusis can be seen in several ways in psychoanalysis. In addition to the rites of procession and cleansing, the mask of Dionysus, god of possession, serves as an emblem of the "loosening" and "maddening" effect of the gathering of energies brought about in the psychoanalytic endeavor (analysis—*loosening, tearing apart*). The labyrinthine procession is analogous to the "night sea journey" through the underworld and its travails reflecting the overall process of the encounter with the unconscious and the reintegration that occurs as a result. "Meandering" is the "serpentine" pattern of the analytic process. Passing an object back and forth between two containers can be seen as indicative of the integration of conscious with unconscious life, as well as the unconscious transfer of contents in the transference/countertransference relationship of analyst and patient. Seeds represent differentiation of psychic contents into distinct potentials and the winnowing fan, the separation of the wheat from the chaff. A sacred marriage is representative of the joining of oppositional aspects of the psyche that seemed irreconcilable, and the resulting epiphany of new life signified through a flash of light represents new life as an "in-sight" or "recognition" that emerges out of a psychological darkness or confusion. The therapeutic goal is a matter of realignment of personality such that a different perspective or attitude emerges, and an identity is realized and seen as if for the first time.

The Orphic mysteries are a third set of rituals from ancient Greece that reflect healing rituals universally and can be seen as early precedents to psychoanalysis. These are rites of rebirth that are associated with the myths of Zeus and of Dionysus wherein Zeus was dismembered by the Titans but reborn, and Dionysus was dismembered and reborn from the thigh of Zeus. Orpheus himself was mythically dismembered and reborn over and over as the ritual substitute for Dionysus. These rites include a sense of original sin through a confession of guilt at offending the divine order. The *mystei* or attendants known as *therapeutei*, had a therapeutic function in that they served as a form of "alter ego" upon whom impurities were cast. They were denied certain foods and pleasures, covered in lime and plaster and placed in a painful position in which they were ritually beaten with branches as if dismembered. They were in effect turned into figures of the *pharmakos* or ritual scapegoat with punishment of the body, the tomb of the soul, vetted out as a means of atonement and transformation into a new source of life. Finally, there was a triumphant "Dance of the *Kouretes*" reenacting the mythical Kouretes dance around the twice-born infant Zeus to the sound of clanging swords and shields in protection of the child from the Titans. As part of the ecstatic dance, the god himself was invited to join in, to "leap for the ships," "leap for the cities," and "leap for flocks and fields." The new life is accomplished in the context of unity with the collective group and in conjunction with the divine.

The assault on the body enacted in these rites as a form of dismemberment and atonement of guilt might be seen in psychoanalysis as the psychological loosening of defensive structures and in conjunction with the denial of social and physical gratification that inevitably arises in the relationship of analyst and patient. Psychoanalysis sees the need for this boundary to maintain a reflective stance toward instinctual needs as they arise in order to integrate them into the psyche as a whole. Ritual scapegoating can be seen in the transference relationship of patient to analyst as well as in the patient's internal identification with his/her guilt and the turn to aggression upon the self. Finally, the Dance of the *Kouretes* can be considered as the attitude of honoring the world outside of analysis that is mutually shared by analyst and patient alike and which provides a cultural container for the analytic process.

Generic Native Healing Rituals

In looking into healing practices across different native cultures, certain rituals tend to appear ubiquitously in the process of contending with external forces. One theme that frequently occurs is that of *extraction*, an appeal to the gods to remove that which is causing distress. A possessing evil spirit may be drawn out through exorcism, in which case the spirit is evoked and compelled to exit through the authority of the healer and the ritual action of blowing it out, sucking and spitting it out, or casting it into a scapegoated animal. Extraction through literal sucking out of an object such as a human tooth or a bloody worm from the body of the patient is analogous to the analyst's teasing out of an underlying conflict or complex through focus upon painful issues which have been covered over. Giving them up is inevitably vigorously resisted by the patient. One can see in psychoanalysis a dynamic like exorcism in the power of suggestion carried by imagination that works in the transference or "throwing out" of an unwanted content by a patient onto the analyst or in the act of ventilating or regurgitating emotion with words.

Another mode of extraction in native cultures is through the ritual of confession, the "expression" of feelings of guilt. The confessor takes on the aspect of a "containing authority" such as a sacred rock, a river, a totem animal, an ancestor, a holy man or the entire collective of family, clan or tribe. The confession has to do with the neglect of ancestors or a breach of "taboo," a word which comes out of Polynesian usage meaning "prohibited," "disallowed," or "forbidden," but also comes from certain African uses referring to the literal "place or ground of destruction." In the African tribe, the Ndembu, a literal root (getting to the root of the problem) embodying an offended ancestor is dug up to be addressed. Confession is a mode of "catharsis," a word which comes from ancient Greek use meaning "cleansing or purging" involving release of emotional tension. In psychoanalysis, "abreaction" comes from the recall of a memory, feeling, idea or fantasy and its elimination through giving it expression. In cults such as peyote cults, a form of confession is induced by ritual vomiting followed by intense weeping. In psychoanalysis, the entire enterprise of acknowledging one's sense of limitations, a kind of head "shrinking," takes on the aspect of confession.

A ritual dynamic counter to extraction in that it involves receiving, is the "blessing," the calling upon a beneficent power giving the patient a "new life" from outside sources. Here the sacrifice works as an attractor, "I give, that you may give." Most often this is brought about by bringing the patient into physical contact with an object of spiritual power such as a fetish, like a sacred string of knots or circular object, a natural object like a sacred stone or crystal, the incisor of an ancestor, a powder of mixed herbs, bark and plant leaves, a sacred food, or the head or shell or blood of a sacrificed animal, all giving forth power through contact with the patient's body. Additionally, blessing is brought about through the taking in of an emetic or sacred drink or the rite of fumigation, the breathing in (the term "soul" originally connoted "breath") of the smoke from the burning of a sacred plant. Being brushed with objects such as leaves associated with ancestors and divinities brings the patient into right alignment with family and cosmos. Finally, the outside influence may come directly through language itself in blessings and incantations for the patient. One can see reflected in all of these rituals evoking outside healing powers the practices in psychoanalysis connecting the patient with self-healing energies which have been repressed thereby bringing about a realignment of psychic structure.

Shamanic Healing

The shamanic mode of native healing can be seen to have its complement in certain aspects of psychoanalysis. The major qualities of shamanic healing and their reflections in psychoanalysis are as follows:

1) The shaman goes into a deliberate trance, in which he leaves the here-and-now of the everyday world. Analysts don't go into trances, but they do "fall" into a special state of consciousness in which they can hear the patient in a deeper metaphorical way than a literalistic mode of listening would permit. We call this mode of hearing "reverie," evoking a liminal space that allows for

reverberations, fantasies, and feelings to make their appearance within the therapist.

2) The shaman takes an ecstatic journey to the edges of the universe—the highs of the heavens or the lows of the underworld. The state of reverie in psychoanalysis allows for a kind of psychological movement that can have highs and lows, darkness and light which is shared by patient and analyst in an underlying co-created imaginal space of inter-relationship or "subtle body."

3) The climax of the journey is the confrontation with the spirit that has taken the soul of the patient, often involving a battle, which is necessary in order to retrieve the patient's soul. The confrontation with the unconscious is the aspect of psychoanalysis wherein, once a repressed content has been teased out by the analyst's careful interventions, both analyst and patient can begin and continue the process of dialogue *with* that painful content or unwanted feeling resulting in its gradual integration.

4) The shaman may in some manner "take in" the disease and suffer a dismemberment along with a successive regathering of his body as a renewal. Likewise, the shaman might ingest the evil spirit for the sake of gaining control over it, eventually expelling it through means such as regurgitation. This is reflected in the aspect of the analytic endeavor wherein the analyst psychologically takes in the patient's unwanted feelings and presents them in a way that is tolerable to the patient.

5) The shaman will often take on an animal form as a means of incarnating an ancestral or totemic presence. In psychoanalysis, this is the attitude of the therapist in accepting or *taking on* the character, negative or idealized, that the patient imagines him/her to be. The analyst allows him/herself to be used by the patient, thereby becoming a certain necessary object in the patient's psychological life. When the analyst takes on this character, it can be mutually reflected upon and integrated resulting in a new alignment.

6) Once a soul is retrieved by the shaman, it is reintroduced into the patient by means such as literally blowing it into the patient's lungs. In psychoanalysis the self-healing power of the patient's psyche, its "re-ensoulment," is evoked by the analyst's basic assumption that ultimately the patient always has the power to take responsibility for his/her choices. Here the analyst is consistently pointing out the existential fact of individual responsibility for choices which can then be explored.

7) The symbol that is most often associated with the shaman is the drum representing cosmic rhythms through the different levels of the universe—underworld, earth, sky—corresponding to different levels of consciousness. In psychoanalysis, the drum would be the analyst's sensitivity to the rhythm of the process, slow and steady, rapid and passionate, reflecting the varying vibrations or the heartbeat of the analytic relationship itself.

Rituals of Ndembu

As we have seen previously, anthropologist Victor Turner has studied and written extensively on rituals performed by the Zambian Ndembu tribe.[2] The Ndembu word for ritual literally means "to blaze a trail," and Turner takes up the progressive process of ritual laid out in Arnold van Gennep's description of rites of passage as 1) separation, 2) marginalization, and 3) aggregation. In separation the subject is excluded from the ongoing daily structures of society through symbolic techniques such as burial, physical expulsion, or confinement to a hut.

It is the second stage that is most interesting to Turner, what he calls liminality. Liminality is a physical and psychological space where the normalizing ongoing structures and hierarchies of societies are given over to *communitas* or an order of equalization of values of all things and figures. Those values and personages that are normally high in a society are reviled and brought down and those normally low are raised to a dominant position. Inferiority of being, weakness, humility are brought about by stripping away all vestige of normative existence. Paradox reigns as the line between dualities such as life/death, male/female, light/dark, and animal/human becomes blurred and ambiguous. The subject, at once, is both alive and dead and not alive or dead, neither male nor female and both male and female. The spirits of ancestors become present as family and community fade away. Cultural norms are turned upside down such that what is habitual for one gender becomes a *modus operandi* for the other or a fall from a tree is ritualistically invited and set up around a tree with actual slippery bark.

In one ritual, two holes are dug and a tunnel bored underground between them. One hole is ordained to represent life, the other, death. A male fire is built above ground on one side of the tunnel below and a female fire on the other. The patient enters the hole of life, traverses the tunnel and emerges at the hole of death and then returns through the tunnel to emerge from the hole of life renewed. The ritual brings together states of being: animal and human, male and female, above and below, life and death. Turner sees ritual as providing an overall sensibility to existence as governed by forces ultimately beyond human control, but which can be conjured up and related to through the container of ritual.

In Turner's analysis and descriptions, one can see an analogy to psychoanalysis as ritual. The patient enters a space separated physically and psychologically through the rules of confidentiality from the outer world. The patient is put in a position of comfortable yet vulnerable physicality and deprived of persona-restoration through social interaction with the analyst. The relationship of analyst/patient is of a completely different order of interaction than that of everyday life, focused as it is on finding meaning in all facets of the patient's psychic life including the analytic interaction. In this space anything can be evoked, talked about and given equal consideration and value no matter how disgusting, frightening, or "other" to ego consciousness of the day world. Through reliving and reconnecting with darkly unwanted aspects of psychic life and experiencing them through personal and archetypal meaning, the patient is able to reenter daily life in a more wholistic, transformed, albeit not predictable or ego syntonic, regathered way.

Rituals of Navajo Healing[3]

For the Navajo, the rituals of healing take on an especially central part of cultural life. The practice of healing is indistinguishable from the practices of art, entertainment and religion. The healer is, at once, a painter, singer, and priest, as well as a doctor. He paints astoundingly complex images with multicolored sands, sings from memory elaborate chants that last for hours, and is intermediary with the gods. Religious ceremonies are predominately healing rituals which involve and heal not only the individual patient, but the clan of the patient, as well as the entire community. The mythical heroes of the Navajo learned secrets of healing from both the gods and from the legendary enemies. The foundational stories that tell how the cosmos, world, and culture came into being are means of healing.

What heals for the Navajo is a realignment with the patterns of the universe. Unlike shamanic healing and its identification through trance with supernatural powers, Navajo healing requires the fully conscious utilization of a complex knowledge system and its techniques of symbolization to bring about order through ritual. The ceremonies are arranged and paid for by the family of the patient, and those more elaborate are quite expensive, take a good deal of preparation, and ultimately involve the entire community. The preparations include engaging the services of both diagnostician and medicine man or singer, preparing the ceremonial hut or *hogan*, providing for firewood, water, and food for several days, and arranging for the appearance of dancers. There are many ceremonies, each with their own set of chants, sand paintings and rituals, all to be performed perfectly for the ceremony to be effectual. Each ceremony and singer is "specialized;" each ceremony meant for only certain maladies and based on a different set of myths related to those maladies. Each singer is trained in only a few ceremonies, each one requiring years of training to be performed properly.

The main intention of the ceremony is to bring the patient into harmony with world order through application of symbols in chant, sandpainting image, and ritual. Navajo rituals are conducted in huts that have been consecrated as a sacred space where humans may encounter the divine. An individual with symptoms wanting treatment goes to a diagnostician -a hand trembler or gazer into crystals, stars, embers, or animal entrails – who ascertains the problem and its cause and refers to a "singer" who is knowledgeable in that illness and the prescribed ceremony.

The master of the ceremony is called the singer. The patient and family go to the singer and arrive at an acceptable fee and date for the ceremony, certain ceremonies being possible only during specific times of the year. Ritualized preparations are conducted, and the ceremony is launched. Mythic stories, often lasting hours, are "sung" in a word-perfect chant by the singer serving to identify the patient with his/her mythic origins and cosmic order, to bless the patient with the influence of positive forces, to protect the patient from evil influences, and to bring the patient into linguistic identification with beneficent figures for the sake of wellbeing or maleficent figures for the sake of exorcism.

The most visually spectacular aspects of the Navajo rituals are the sand paintings created by the singer on the floor of the ceremonial *hogan*. These depictions ranging in size from 1½ to 12 feet in diameter depict symbols, gods and sacred animals in arrangements depicting cosmic order as expressed in myths which are the foundations of the ceremony. The patient generally sits on the painting and thus is brought into identification with a transcendent order which extends to the community as well. In some Navaho ceremonials, the sense of return to origins by repeating acts of the gods is literally enacted when the patient ritualistically walks in the steps of a god such as Corn Boy, as depicted in the sandpainting, analogous to the psychoanalytic patient proceeding by steps through life's past events.

In the Navajo ceremony, Nine Night Chant, there are several smaller rituals that can be seen as reflective of actions in psychoanalysis. The patient is cleansed by the singer with a special kind of suds made from the yucca plan, a form of "psychic baptism," which characterizes an initial supportive stance by the analyst. It is also symbolic of the ongoing therapeutic process of "working through," "coming clean," alchemical *solutio*, regurgitating painful material over and over until its potency is lessened, bringing into the open the festering influence of psychological impurities such as shame and guilt. The Navajo patient spends a period of time in a sweat lodge soaking in the steam of a sweat bath. This event reflects a process of psychic heating in psychoanalysis when the patient, momentarily "on the hot seat," is confronted by feelings that have been repressed and undergoes a kind of shrinking experience when subjectivity experienced through the self that has been falsely created becomes diminished.

The ceremony continues over several days. During the second day, the patient is covered with spruce branches, literally bound "up tight," which are then ritualistically cut away. This would be analogous to the activation, analysis, and integration of various defenses or misguided scripts appearing in the context of psychoanalysis. During the fourth day, a mask is fastened to the head of the patient by the figure of a god and then fastened to a live spruce which has been bent over. The spruce is then "sprung" by another god-figure, pulling the mask off the patient as the tree jerks back into an upright position. This is like the event in analysis when the patient realizes a "false self" has been adopted for defensive purposes and a more authentic "face" is available.

A sacred talisman is applied to different parts of the patient's body by the singer, just as in psychoanalysis various psychological aspects of the patient are "touched" by the analyst's inquiries. The talisman is then unraveled before the patient, enacting the teasing out of a complex in an analysis. A sacred material is lit, and the patient breathes in the smoke in an act of fumigation, again analogous to the analytic patient "breathing in" the enabling influences of the analytic encounter such as the ability to hold and reflect upon emotions. An emetic is given to the patient to drink in blessing, something like the analytic patient's "introjection" of the empathic attitude of the analyst or realizing beneficent attitudes toward the self from internal sources. The mask of a god is fastened to the patient's face while blindfolded and then the blindfold removed, allowing for the patient to gain the "sight of the gods," or in psychoanalysis, to gain an "insight."

Finally, on the last night of the ceremony which has lasted nine nights, masked and costumed gods appear and dance for the patient, again bringing the patient and community into identification with origins in myth and bestowing blessings. Toward dawn the singer comes to a section of the chant in which he relates how the bluebirds are singing to each other at dawn. This event occurs at the time when bluebirds are actually singing to each other in the environs outside of the ceremonial hut indicating the connection of the ceremony with the actuality of the world. This would be similar to the analytic patient's venture into the world, in harmony with a capacity to affect that world in his/her own way.

To reiterate the connection between psychoanalysis and Navajo ritual, in analysis image and its feeling tone manifest through memory and imagination. The analytic patient "works through" events of past, present, and potential future life in language, now emerging in a realm separated from the world of everyday life. In the telling of stories and fantasies, the patient puts him or herself into an existence of a different order, that of the liminal space between dayworld reason and the reality of the imaginal world. At the same time, as the patient is re-imagining his or her life, lived and dormant, larger patterns emerge which have been unconsciously reenacted over and over and can now be seen. Dreams also reveal the visitation of larger-than-life, mysterious figures and patterns.

As the analysis proceeds, these images become more discernible as split-off part objects of the patient's personality which in their unconscious form take on the power and aspect of divinities, those which drain and those which provide psychic energy. In short, the patient sees how he/she creates contemporary reality under the influence of figures and patterns from another world, the unconscious. Whereas these patterns and figures are initially experienced as being products of a personal life, they can also eventually be seen as universal, thereby connecting the individual to a universal consciousness. In sum, we might say that the primary mode of psychoanalysis, the use of imagination to ritualistically return to origins to recover concealed aspects of the personal and universal psyche, is analogous to the rituals of Navajo healing which literally enact a return and identification with origins to bring about a proper personal and universal psychological alignment.

Western Ritual Antecedents to Psychoanalysis[4]

The first overt, mainstream pre-figuration of psychoanalysis in the West can be seen in the practice of exorcism performed on the general population in the late 1770's by a German country priest, Father John Gassner (1727-1779). Gassner would induce a crisis, exhorting the devil dwelling in the body of the patient to manifest itself through symptoms in various parts of the body. If the symptoms appeared, Gassner would expel the evil spirit. If symptoms did not appear, he would refer the patient to a medical practitioner. Here we can see the precursor to the psychoanalytic ritual of evoking the psychic conflict and transforming it through therapeutic interpretation and integration.

Practicing in the Age of Enlightenment with its emphasis on reason and science, Gassner was opposed by many, one of whom was to establish the next technique leading to psychoanalysis, the Viennese physician Anton Messmer (1734-1815). Messmer took the practice of autosuggestion completely out of the realm of religion and applied what he thought of as scientific technique, which presupposed a transpersonal energy, to the cure of patients. Messmer believed that there was an invisible fluid running throughout the universe acting as a connector between humans, the earth and heavenly bodies. He thought that symptoms of disease appear in humans when there is an unequal distribution of this fluid in the body, and they can be cured with a redistribution that would achieve an overall equilibrium. It is possible, Mesmer maintained, to manipulate this fluid when a crisis is evoked, and proper techniques are applied with the use of magnets.

Mesmer began by giving his patient a preparation containing iron and attaching magnets to the patient's body. The patient would then experience extraordinary streams of fluid running down through the body. Messmer believed that it was the proportionate distribution of the fluid in his own body, with the magnet acting as mediator, that brought about the curative realignment in the patient's body. He called this effect "animal magnetism" (*animus* being the Latin word for "breath.") He later used a magnet that he passed over the induced bleeding of the patient or a stick or a vessel known as *baquet* for several patients at once. Eventually, he was able to produce a similar effect by sitting in front of his seated patient, knee to knee, pressing the patient's thumbs in his hands, requesting the patient look intently into his eyes and then touching various parts of his own body, or passing his hand in front of the patient bringing about the curative realignment in the patient.

Messmer maintained that his theory and technique were entirely within the realm of science and in particular, the field of electricity. What is important for our purposes is to note the auto-suggestive role that he himself played in the curative process. In sum, here we have the prefiguration to the concept of "psychic energy" and its realignment as the goal of psychoanalysis, as well as the suggestive influence of the "touch" of the analyst in the transference/ countertransference interrelationship with the patient.

The next step leading to the invention of free association and psychoanalysis was the advent of hypnotism by one of Mesmer's disciples, the Marquis de Puysegur (1751-1825), a military officer and country gentleman who experimented with electricity. Puysegur learned Mesmerism from a brother and found that he could induce in the peasants who came to him for treatment a "perfect crisis" of symptoms. Within a kind of waking state, the patient would not only follow his suggestions but then forget the entire healing episode in its aftermath. In other words, the event was similar to sleepwalking, an "artificial somnambulism." In addition, Puysegur was impressed by the lucidity with which patients were able to diagnose and treat themselves, thus introducing the aspect of self-awareness and the self-healing power of the psyche. Above all, Puysegur emphasized that it was not so much a physical fluid but the will and belief of the "magnetizer," in other words the rapport that was able to bring about the successful treatment. Again, we see the importance of the quality of ritualized relationship between patient and doctor that serves as a healing agent in psychoanalysis.

Abbe' Faria, a Portuguese priest living in Paris but formerly of India, shifted focus from the magnetizer to the suggestibility of the subject. He would command the subject to sleep and then induce visions and posthypnotic suggestions. The inventor of "hypnosis" per se was the Scottish surgeon James Baird who, following the teachings and practices of Eastern meditation and yoga, held that the effective agency in producing a cure through trance was the capacity of the subject to focus all consciousness on a single point. Faria's and Baird's theories and work eventually led to a burgeoning of clinical interest in hypnosis as a tool for treatment. Among the foremost clinics and hospitals utilizing hypnosis were the Nancy School under the leadership of Hippolyte Bernheim, (who made the term "psychotherapeutics" standard after Walter Deady had earlier coined the term "psychotherapeia,") and the Salpetriere School under Jean Martin Charcot. Each of these were study grounds for Sigmund Freud who moved from hypnosis as a treatment to free association and the invention of psychoanalysis. The technique of hypnosis can be considered as a precursor to the condition of reverie or the "imaginal world" that is brought about in psychoanalysis.

The same thinking and techniques practiced ritualistically in a religious setting across cultures and through the ages emerged in a secular form in the Western world of Europe in the late 18th and 19th Centuries. Although ancient and native cultures have tended to literalize what psychoanalysis takes metaphorically, the common themes of liminal space as place of healing, the need to confront a larger-than-life causative force, the evocation of the dis-ease itself to be addressed, and the power of the relationship between healer and patient to heal, are universal. What native and ancient cultures see in terms of a transcendent or divine world, psychoanalytic psychotherapy sees in terms of the "unconscious." The container for all of this, ritual, emerges as itself the healer, ritual in service to a psychodynamic return to origins and realignment of psychic energy.

If ritual is the instinctual action to bring about change in relations to larger-than-life forces as a means of healing, what emerged from ritual was a narrative or story to amplify and give structure to the cosmic order out of which the ritual emerges. This narrative, we would call myth. In sum, out of ritual emerged myth, and one of the emergent factors in the focus on ritual as healer is the power of myth itself to heal. In the next chapter, we shall look further into the mythic aspect of healing, myth as healer.

Out of Act emerges Story . . .

Endnotes

[1] Hartigan K., *Performance and Cure: Drama and Healing in in Ancient Greece and Contemporary America*; Meier, C., *Ancient Incubation and Modern Psychotherapy*; Kerenyi, C., Eleusis: Archetypal Image of Mother and Daughter.

[2] Turner, V., *The Forest of Symbols: Aspects of Ndembu Ritual*, and *The Ritual Process*.

[3] Sandner, D., *Navaho Symbols of Healing*.

[4] Ellenberger, H., *The Discovery of the Unconscious*.

Chapter Five

Myth as Guide/Wound as Healer

"The wounded surgeon plies the steel
That questions the distempered part;
Beneath the bleeding hands we feel
The sharp compassion of the healer's art

Resolving the enigma of the fever chart

Our only health is the disease
If we obey the dying nurse
Whose constant care is not to please
But to remind of our, and Adam's curse,
And that, to be restored, our sickness must grow
worse."

-T. S. Eliot, "East Coker"

"In these lay a great multitude of impotent folk, of blind, halt, withered, waiting for the moving of the water. For an angel went down at a certain season into the pool and troubled the water: whosoever then first after the troubling of the water stepped in was made whole of whatsoever disease he had."

-John 5:3-4

"I kill, and I make alive; I wound, and I heal . . ."

-Deuteronomy 32:39

"We learn, further, that Sulphur, is not only the '*medicina*' but also the '*medicus*'—the wounded physician."

-C. G. Jung, *Mysterium Coniunctionis*, Par.144

71

In his book, *The Fifty Minute Hour*, the psychoanalyst Robert Lindner, tells the story of working with a schizophrenic patient. The patient was under the delusion that he was a heroic leader in an extraterrestrial world. This world was very complicated, having its own history, architecture, art, sciences, geography, etc. In the process of creating a bond of rapport with his patient, Lindner describes joining with him in studying maps of the cosmos, creating timelines of history, and working out complex schedules of when and where different events might occur throughout this imaginal universe. Lindner eventually became so taken by this project that he found himself possessed by the desire to figure out the workings of his patient's universe independent of his patient. It was as if he, as doctor, had taken on his patient's disease. One day his patient came into the office for a scheduled session and declared to Lindner, "I've been lying to you . . . making it all up . . . I saw through all that stuff-weeks ago . . . I realized I was crazy, deluding myself for years."[1] By giving up his own universe and showing concern for the doctor's belief in his fantasy, the patient indicated that he had developed the capacity for relationship with another person. Because the doctor had taken on and held the patient's disease himself, the patient was able to integrate other aspects of his personality.

This story brings up the question of the nature of healing, and what is the relationship between two concepts that are usually thought of as being separate and opposed, wounding and healing. In psychotherapy, the self/other configuration is formed around a double dynamic of wounding and healing as they circle around and through the dyad of doctor/patient.[2] Jess Groesbeck has offered a hypothetical, hierarchal scheme of psychological dynamics at work between doctor and patient.[3] At the surface level doctor and patient relate to each other as wounded and healer. Doctor has knowledge and power by virtue of certified station, patient is rendered with less agency by his/her wounds. Patient needs doctor, doctor needs patient. Doctor is well, in conjunction with patient as ill. Beneath this dynamic is the level of personal wounds held by both doctor and patient.

The doctor's healing power is secretly being activated by wounds, while the wounds of the patient are being acted upon by an underlying self-healing power. The wounds of the doctor find their expression in the patient as does the healing power of the patient find itself in the doctor. Healing takes place to the extent that doctor can become aware of the wounds on his/her side while patient becomes aware of the power of self-healing on his/her side. Underneath the personal wounds of both doctor and patient lies the archetypal image or realm of the interrelated wounded/healer configuration from which the process as a whole is activated and the psyches of both doctor and patient are energized. We can then suggest that the fundamental ethics of the psychotherapeutic enterprise is the capacity to consciously differentiate what the patient wants, what the therapist wants, and what the relationship or the "work" (*opus*) of mutual engagement wants.

In summary, wounding and healing, disease and cure, paradoxically appear very much as interactive parts of the same universal configuration. The archetypal perspective suggests the following ideas to consider:

1) Healing occurs by way of a healer, who is wounded.

2) That aspect of the healer which brings about healing is the healer's wound.

3) The healer can only heal if she/he has proper relationship to her/his wound.

4) Effort to heal others has the double function of being an attempt to heal self.

5) The wound of the healer is what brings her/him into the healing profession.

Healing Approaches

When we speak of healing, we can distinguish between two different modes of healing. Allopathic healing uses elements foreign to the disease to produce effects different from those of the disease. When mental distress is treated with psychiatric medication, behavioral techniques, or directives, something alien to the disease is being introduced to eliminate the symptoms. When we treat headaches from stress with biofeedback, we are introducing something alien, sound waves, to get rid of pain. By contrast, homeopathic healing involves an agent *like* the disease producing effects similar to the disease. A vaccination is an introduction of a slight form of the disease itself so that the body will build up agents to combat a more potent form of the disease. An old saying goes, "like cures like." In psychotherapy, initial sources of psychic pain are evoked and revisited through a mutual exploration of the feelings and associations which underlie the patient's present experience including his/her relationship with the therapist. During therapy, these feelings are worked through and integrated, allowing the patient a new experience of him or herself. Therapy is then based upon the sensibility that sickness carries within itself the power to heal.

Allopathy and homeopathy represent two fundamental approaches toward healing, each representing a base of assumptions and ways of seeing. Psychotherapy can be considered as an expression of the "wounded healer" revealed in the healing rituals of cultures universally. The ancient Greeks believed illness is caused by divinity and therefore could only be cured by divinity. The oracle of Apollo declared, "He who wounds also heals." In Babylon, a dog goddess had two names: as "Gula" she was death, and as "Labartu" she was healing. In India, Kali is goddess of the pox and its healer. Healing is an event associated with a religious attitude which regards the god as the sickness and the remedy at the same time. The paradox in this idea is indicative of a depth of expression we can refer to as "mythic."

Myth

Myths convey the original patterns of human existence. The word means "story" and myths tell stories of the movement of consciousness through different psychological realms. Myths address the question not so much of why, but, where, from whence, toward what goal. Myths present themselves as image, taking us out of the literal and into the imaginal realm, giving rise to imagination as the appropriate mode of addressing psychological life. Myths form the ground, the "ur" or "archai," the original patterns of human existence.

Myths are also what cannot be spoken. The word *mythos* is connected to words that mean mute, mum, mumble, mutter, and mystery. The Sanskrit *muka* means dumb. So, myths have something to do with that which cannot be spoken and is beyond us. Relative to the insight of both Freud and Jung, myths tell us that they *have us* in every instant of consciousness. Myths are not just old stories, but active and alive in the present. There is always a journey or a creation or a battle or the deeds of gods occurring in our daily perceptions, thoughts, fantasies, feelings, and actions. Myths are that through which we meet and know the world, presenting us to the world and the world to us. Myths are styles of being with the world, and they tell us that the gods are alive, the divine at work and play, in every human moment. Through mythic consciousness, we sense that something else is going on outside of our concerns and knowledge.

Joseph Campbell, the teacher and writer who did much to bring myth into the public imagination, talked about myth in four ways which we can see, for example, in comparing Western and Navajo Native American cultures. Myths have a metaphysical function in that they connect us with the larger-than-life mysteries. In the Western world, God's divine love or wrath, or the logic of reason and science, or the ubiquitous dynamics of economy—all at one time or another are or have been seen as the predominant power that makes the world what it is. For the Navajo, by contrast, Beauty is the force that predominates in the world, and it is alignment with beauty that brings health and harmony to the individual and community.

The second feature of myth is the cosmological function. Myths speak to us in images and present us with forms that convey the patterns of the mysteries of the universe. In the Western tradition, the image of Jesus on the cross conveys the image of suffering that will eventually lead to a rebirth. In contemporary times, this mythic image has been translated into the popular figure of the victim with the fundamental story: promise turns to victimhood turns to a rebirth and new possibility. For the Navajo, one of the images that appears in a major ceremonial is that of the whirling logs. This swastika-like pattern is a depiction from a myth in which a hero floats down a river, encountering many adventures until he comes to the place of the gods wherein they are seated on a cross made of logs which are whirling around in the water. In symbolic terms, this is a mandala, a depiction of the central axis of the universe.

Campbell's third function is the sociological function in which myths validate social order. The fundamental code of morality of the Judeo-Christian tradition comes from the myth of Moses and God's Ten Commandments for the Children of Israel. Navajo myths depict the transgressions that make up the cultural taboos which, if broken, give rise to disease and disability. Finally, myth serves what Campbell calls a psychological function by providing the individual a "pathway" through his or her life. In other words, myth serves as a guide with which the individual can navigate through life. The depth psychologist, James Hillman, has referred to this idea as a myth giving us a map of our mess. In American culture, the figure of the hero is the preeminent means of gaining recognition and establishing identity. For the Navajo, myth provides a means of achieving adulthood through various forms of initiation rituals. Girls become women via mythic wandering by going through several days of the *kinalda* ceremony involving running away from home in the company of family and friends. Over the course of several days each run goes further with fewer companions until on the last day she runs by herself and then is welcomed back to the family with a ceremonial cake.

Using these four functions we can see how myth heals in psychotherapy and Navajo healing. The metaphysical function is served in Western psychotherapy by the patient giving over control of consciousness by gaining a sense that ultimately his or her unconscious life is more powerful in determining experience than the choices of his/her subjectivity. In the Navajo world, the metaphysical function is achieved during ceremonies when the individual patient is brought into right alignment with the beauty of the universe through identification with the gods. The cosmological function is served in psychotherapy by looking at the patterns of one's life and seeing in them both personal and universal tendencies. For the Navajo, the cosmologic function is evident in the ceremonial images of the cosmos depicted in the sand paintings upon which the patient sits in literal alignment with images of the cosmos. The sociological function is served in psychotherapy through the morality that psychotherapy brings, namely that the individual has unconsciously created the suffering or the conditions of his or her life that feel so painful. For the Navajo, healing rituals rectify the broken taboos or transgressions of the past which allow healing to take place. Finally, psychotherapy validates the individual path, the distinct form of the individual in the world. Myth recognizes therapy itself as a heroic process of suffering and reemergence to new possibilities. The ceremonies of the Navajo give the patient the opportunity to walk in the steps of the gods, to follow the ways of the gods, and see with the eyes of the gods as a means of living a life in harmony with the cosmic order.

Navajo Myth and Healing

In Navajo mythology, the dominant heroic characters are twin warrior brothers, one of whom, Monster Slayer, brought back knowledge of healing from his encounters with his monster enemies. The warrior twins were complemented in their healing powers by another set of twins whom we have previously met:

The Stricken Twins

A girl from a poor family is approached buy one of the gods, Talking God, who proposes marriage. She resists at first but finally succumbs and ultimately gives birth to twins. In their ninth year, the twins wander off, become trapped among rocks for four days and nights and when they emerge, one is blind, the other lame. They come back to the family with the blind boy carrying the lame on his shoulders and the lame boy guiding the blind. The family is unable to cure them, and when they become too problematic for the family to care for them, the boys are expelled from the family compound.

With council from their father, Talking God, the boys visit a group of gods in hopes of being healed. They are rejected by this set of gods but directed to another where they are again rejected but referred on to another group. This pattern occurs several times. Finally, it becomes clear that they do not have the sacred objects which the gods need and demand as price for treatment. After a circuitous and arduous journey searching in vain for help from the gods and even again from the family, the boys are finally given aid by the council of the gods.

The gods will cure the boys without a payment of sacred objects, but there is one condition the boys must follow: they must not speak until after the ceremony. The cure consists of a sweat bath of intense heat inside a sweat hut. When the heat subsides, the blind boy sees, and the lame boy is able to move his legs. Still inside the hut, they spontaneously exclaim their joy to each other, thereby breaking the taboo and the spell is broken. They revert back to their conditions of blindness and lameness and the gods tell them to leave and not return. The boys leave and wander slowly down the trail, the blind carrying the lame, the lame seeing for the blind. In their despair, they utter sighs and groanings which gradually turn to words, and the words then turn into songs. The gods hear the songs and are pleased and curious about them. They call the boys back and ask them where they learned the beautiful songs. The boys say the songs just come from their cries. The gods are pleased with the songs and change their minds. They give the boys detailed instructions on how to obtain and use helpers—a rat, worm, four grasshoppers and the wind—to obtain three sacred objects for the ceremony. With the aid of their new helpers the boys take a long journey in which they encounter evil powers on the way to obtaining the sacred articles needed for the ceremony. The ceremony is performed with the articles and, as well, the songs that the boys had sung are used in the ceremonial healing. The boys are cured and return to their people with knowledge of healing through rituals, sand paintings, sacred objects and now songs. Out of their woundedness, the twins became healers.

The myth reflects Navajo healing on several levels. It is a story about one of the ways in which healing came to be among the Navajo. It tells of the origin of the first singers and of the chants and songs sung during actual healing ceremonies and how they came about. Finally, the myth tells of rites that are performed to this day for symptoms like those of the boys.

Elements of Western psychotherapy can be detected in the myth. The meandering movement of the boys from one group of gods to another further parallels the circuitous route that healing takes in therapy with its necessary "snake-like" recycling of problems until the time is right for change. The sweat bath can be a metaphor for the therapeutic process itself in that the therapist applies a form of heat by not gratifying either the patient's or the therapist's emotional needs for fusion. This heat then evokes a kind of psychological "sweating" in which unintegrated feelings can be worked through in therapeutic processing. The result is a transformation that involves a kind of "shrinking" of water-logged complexes. As bloated, unconscious contents come to light to be dried out so that a more essential sense of personality emerges.

The myth of the Stricken Twins tells us something of the importance of sacrifice in the therapeutic enterprise. Over and over the boys were told that if they didn't have what the gods needed, they couldn't be treated. Psychologically, there is a giving up of former identity, energy held by underlying complexes, conscious assumptions and expectations, all of which are paradoxically given over only with considerable resistance and discomfort. Symbolic of sacrifice is the fee paid by the patient in that issues may come up in therapy around the fee that reflect the pathology of the patient. The most important sacrifice in psychoanalysis is symbolized by the gifts required by the gods, the giving up of ego control to allow for the emergence of concealed aspects of the personality—rat, worm, grasshoppers and wind.

Each of the four helpers has metaphorical significance for psychotherapy. The rat would be that reviled part of the psyche that inhabits the forgotten and avoided crannies and corners, the interstitial spaces of the personality and survives on the barest of necessities. It is the power wrought from consciousness of these neglected, hidden aspects such as fear, anger, envy, loss that help the patient gain renewed self-awareness. The worm is that life that exists "underground," in the underworld of the psyche, feeding upon the dirt, compost or waste of repressed experience. The grasshopper not only gets us over humps, but represents our instinctual nature, an ability to perceive immediacy, act and react.[4] The wind, for the Navajo, the most powerful element in the universe, can be seen as the spirit or dynamic power of the psyche, that force which is larger than consciousness which motivates and moves the personality.

Most importantly, the myth indicates that it is the experience of being wounded by the family, what we call trauma, that gets the boys underway. In other words, dysfunction and ensuing suffering through separation from all that is customary in terms of identity, community and habitual ways of doing things, is necessary for authentic change to take place. Finally, the journey takes place "blind" and "lame," referring to the fact that the boys are dependent on each other indicative of how "vision" and "action" are, in fact, spontaneously interdependent. Our actions come out of how we see, an attitude of mind, and, at the same time, how we see leads to action. In psychotherapy, the emphasis is upon reflection, seeing, and out of a change in perspective comes a shift in the patient's "vision" of self and resulting mode of action in the world.

Myths of the Ancient Greece and Healing

The stories of the Greek warriors Philoctetes, Telephus, Achilles, and Patroklos tell us that in the background of the archetypal image of the physician and healing is the wound of the warrior.

A) Philoctetes, the snake bitten Greek hero, was left marooned on a desert island by the Greek army on their way to Troy because of the stench of his festering wounds. It was subsequently revealed by prophesy that he was essential for Greek victory over Troy due to his possession of Herakles' weapons. The Greeks, at first reluctant, retrieved the odious warrior. Healed by Machaon, a son of Asklepios the first mortal physician, Philoctetes ultimately turned the tide in their favor.

B) The Greek fleet, while on its way to war in Troy, landed on the shores of the island of Mysia by mistake. Telephus, king of Mysia, led a group of warriors, who were subsequently attacked by the Greeks. Telephus fought off the Greeks but was wounded by Achilles in the thigh. The wound refused to heal. Telephus consulted the oracle of Apollo who told him that only the one who wounded him could be his physician. Dressed in beggar's rags, Telephus sought out Achilles at Agamemnon's palace in Argos. Meanwhile, the Greeks had received an oracle that they could not win the war without Telephus' help. Achilles was willing to heal Telephus, but said he knew nothing of medicine. Odysseus then explained that it was Achilles' spear that had inflicted the wound and, therefore, *it* could act as physician. Achilles scraped rust from the spearhead into the wound, the wound healed, and Telephus guided the Greeks to Troy.

C) Once in battle, the Greek army incurred a series of woundings. The woundings drew the attention of the Greek's greatest warrior, Achilles, who had been holding himself out of the fighting. Asklepios had two sons fighting on the side of the Greeks. One was Podaleirios, who treated invisible wounds, wounds of the soul, thereby becoming the first "psycho-therapist." The other was Machaon, a surgeon, who, having earlier ministered to the Greek leader, Menelaos, became wounded himself. The Greeks were anxious to get Machaon off the battlefield, for as Homer states, "A healer is a man worth many men in his knowledge of cutting out arrows and putting kindly medicines on wounds" (XI, 514-15). Achilles sent his great comrade in arms, Patroklos, to investigate. Patroklos came across Eurypylos, another wounded warrior, took pity on him, tended his wounds, was moved to enter the battle himself and was killed. It was the death of his great friend Patroklos that finally spurred Achilles into the battle and brought about the death of the Trojan leader, Hector. In summary, it was the concrete compassion among warriors, those who do the wounding but who, can also be healers—this compassion caused by a chain of woundings - that finally moved the action of the battle to its conclusion.

In Greek mythology, Asklepios, half mortal, half divine, was the original wounded healer. His mother, Coronis was impregnated by Apollo, the god of healing. Coronis, however, wished to marry another mortal, Ischys, and slept with him. Coronis was subsequently slain by Apollo, who when he saw her on the funeral pyre, was seized with remorse and rescued the infant by Caesarian. birth. Asklepios was brought to life through the flames by his father, Apollo, the god of healing. thereby bringing life to him who had been intended to die.

In another version, Asklepios' mother, Coronis, left him exposed on Mt. Tithion, famous for the medicinal virtues of its plants. There he was nurtured by goats and guarded by a dog. When he was discovered by shepherds, a voice was heard proclaiming that the child would discover every cure for the sick and would awaken the dead. A supernatural light played over the child, so that Asklepios is always considered the offspring of light or fire. This mythic image says that healing is a matter of revelation, something new is discovered. The myth also tells us that one mode of healing occurs in conjunction with discovery and exclamation of speech.

Apollo took the infant Asklepios to Mt. Pelion to be raised by Chiron, king of the centaurs who were half-horse, half human. Chiron was immortal, but once in battle, Hercules, fighting on the side of the centaurs, accidentally wounded him. Because he was immortal, the wound would not heal, and Chiron withdrew to a cave permanently wounded. The cave was an entrance to the underworld, and here Chiron learned the ways of healing with plants and herbs. The mythic image says that in a place of healing possibilities, there is suffering, and that which poisons, also cures. Of Chiron and his relation to healing, Karl Kerenyi writes:

"The half-human, half-theriomorphic god suffers eternally from his wound; he carries it with him to the underworld as though the primordial science that this mythological physician, precursor of the luminous divine physician, embodied for men of later times, were nothing other than the knowledge of a wound in which the healer forever partakes."[5]

The word, "chiron," is the root word for surgery, "with the hand," from the Greek, _chirurgia_, "working with the hands." Apollo healed by stretching his hand over the ill person. In German, the word "to treat" is _behandeln_, "treating with the hands." The word, "chiropractic," comes from Chiron's practice of healing with his hands. Healing, then, is archetypally associated with the laying on of hands, both as in surgery, but also figuratively as in the gentle but precise verbal interventions of the psychotherapist lowering the patient into an unconscious feeling. Paradoxically, the analyst's resisting the temptation to literally reach out and take the hand of the patient is in service to the unfolding psychological process of transformation occurring in the patient.

From Chiron, Asklepios learned the skills of surgery, the ways of the snake, and the use of herbal medicine. Chiron applied the ways of the snake in conjunction with the power of healing which he then taught to Asklepios. Asklepios is often depicted as a snake, and as a snake or "hanging god," he hung Christ-like for three days in a tree. The snake is the traditional symbol of healing because of its keen sight, its connection with the underworld and its ability to rejuvenate itself by casting away its skin.

The staff of Asklepios is a symbolic tree with a snake coiled around it indicating the rational knowledge of Apollo and the instinctual nature of the serpent passed on to humans. In sum, Asklepios was "fathered" by two sides of healing, the rational and the irrational. His birth father was Apollo, a bringer of light and reason who also sent plagues with his far-reaching, poisoned darts. His mentor and adopted father was Chiron, perpetually wounded half animal, half-god, who carried the mystery of chthonic darkness and irrationality.

Asklepios' story finds its terminus when Athene gave him two vials of blood from the body of the gorgon Medusa, a monster with a head of snakes who could turn onlookers instantly to stone. The blood from the left side had the power to raise the dead, that from the right would instantly kill, giving Asklepios the power of life and death. He raised so many from the dead that Hades complained to Zeus that his power was being depleted. Zeus then killed Asklepios with his thunderbolt but later resurrected him and made him a god.

Myth and Shamanic Healing

The shaman is a diseased individual who has gone through a process of healing his own infirmity, and out of this process, learned the power of healing. Shamanic ritual practices illustrate the mythic wounded healer. Among the Yakut natives in Siberia, one destined to become a shaman goes through a phase of being frenzied or epileptoid, losing consciousness, withdrawing to forests, feeding on bark, flinging oneself into water and fire, and wounding oneself with knives. Initiation into shamanism becomes the cure for this condition, and thereafter the budding shaman uses these practices, now under his control, to bring about healing. Another initiatory practice for the Yakut shaman is to go into a ritual death, hibernate for three days in a hut and then reconstitute himself.

Among the Tungus, a future shaman must fall ill and have his body cut into pieces and his blood drunk by souls of dead shamans. A Tungu shaman related how he had fallen ill, and his ancestors pierced him with arrows until he lost consciousness. Then they cut off his flesh, tore out his bones and counted them. If they were all there, they would be reconnected, and he could become a shaman. In the Navajo Flint Way myth and ritual, Gila Monster is shamanic in that he has himself cut up and then restored as a means of healing the patient. A pattern emerges of ritual dismemberment, incubation and realignment.

Shamanic practices suggest the central mythic wounded healer in the Western tradition is Jesus. Malachi prophesies Jesus' coming as a divine healer, ". . . unto you that fear my name shall the sun of righteousness arise with healing in his wings."[6] During his life, Jesus performed many healing miracles. A man came to him and said his son was epileptic, the Greek translation being "moonstruck," that he had fits and kept falling about, often into fire, often into water. The disciples had been unsuccessful in curing the boy. Jesus bade the father to bring the boy to him and he cast out the evil spirit from his body. On another occasion, when Jesus came ashore in the land of Gersenes opposite Galilee, a man possessed by devils came to him. He had not worn clothes nor lived in a house but stayed among tombs. When he saw Jesus, he cried out, "What do you want with me?" Jesus conversed with the devils and gave them leave to depart the man's body and enter a herd of pigs. A woman who had been hemorrhaging for twelve years, touched the edge of Jesus' cloak when he was in a crowd. He asked who had touched him because he had felt the power leave him. She fell on her knees and confessed that she had been the one and her bleeding had stopped. A man whose daughter had just died came to Jesus. He went to the girl and bid for her to rise. Jesus then called his disciples and gave them power and authority to heal, and healing became an essential part of the Christian religious tradition.

These stories indicate metaphorically that Jesus himself was a form of moonstruck boy, man possessed by devils living without clothes among tombs, bleeding woman, and dead girl. He went off by himself into the desert, his crucifixion was a form of dismemberment, he was dead for three days in a sealed off area and then arose again. He jumped into fire and water like the shamans in the sense that he was considered the new light, the fiery "sun of righteousness." He was intricately connected to Mary, whose symbol was the moon which is, in turn, associated with watery "moon dew" and lunacy. Jesus was possessed of a message that seemed heretical to the established priestly mind and in anger knocked over the tables of the money changers at the temple. He railed against hypocrisy of the Pharisees, and declared, "I have not come to bring peace, but a sword. For I have come to set a man against his father and a daughter against her mother . . . and a man's foes will be those of his own household."[7] He was at once the divine physician and the lunatic or mad man. Jesus' hemorrhaging reflected not only his bleeding on the cross, but the suffering entailed in being an unwelcome prophet in his own land. Like the daughter, he arose from the dead, not only after his crucifixion, but over and over again in his turning conventional meaning upside down in parables and paradoxical sayings.

Medieval Myth and Healing

The myth of Jesus as wounded healer carried forward into the Middle Ages. In a medieval legend, the cup known as the Holy Grail, used by Christ at the Last Supper and used to catch some of the blood from his wounds, was kept at a certain magical castle guarded by an order of knights. It came to pass that the king of the castle became wounded in the thigh or hip in battle. He was known as the Fisher King because one of his descendants fed many people with a single fish in imitation of Christ. The wound refused to heal, and the country became a desolate waste land, a condition explicitly connected to the king's wound. Although the spear which wounded the king was kept in the castle, along with the Grail and other sacred objects, the healing of the king could only be accomplished by someone who not only found the magical castle but who asked the correct question. Parcifal, the Perfect Fool, is revealed as the rightful hero when he asks, "Whom does the Grail serve?" The answer to this question was the king himself, so again, the focus is brought not only back to the wound of the king as its own healing agent, but to verbal expression as healer. In some versions of the story, Parcifal heals the king by catching the spear that had wounded the king and bringing it back to the king as the healing agent.[8]

The Paradox of the Wounded Healer

The sense of the archetype of wounded healer underlying the therapeutic event gives rise to several disconcerting images. "Analysis" is a deconstructive action in that the root of the word means to "undo," "loosen," or "tear apart." This action is one which must affect the therapist as well as the patient, opening up doctor and patient to the gap between what is known and what is not known. The therapist becomes something of a diver fishing for octopus by allowing him or herself to go down to the bottom of the lagoon, become entangled in the octopus and then pulled up by fellow fishermen. Or like the native crocodile hunter, who allows himself to become the bait for the croc and then is pulled ashore so that it can be captured in its pursuit by his comrades. The therapist figuratively "takes in" the disease of the patient analogous to the honey badger which takes in the cobra's poison and then swallows the cobra or to Catherine of Sienna who drank a cup of pus to show her faith in the healing power of God thereby indicating the sustaining power within decay. Tears can be considered from the standpoint of the wounded healer as expressing their own patterns of "beauty" in the bitter salts of experience which have sustained the soul. When a patient dreams of his therapist as being sick and hot with a fever, while the patient is cold and covered, it can be understood as alluding to the therapist's holding of the secret anger of the patient toward the therapist.

The ancient Greek sensibility of the paradoxical connection between wounding and healing can be seen in the roots of the word "pharmacy." Chiron's medicinal plants were the original *pharmakon*, herbs as drugs which both caused and cured disease. The Greek word *pharmakon* refers to "remedy," but also to "poison." The *pharmakos* is a "scapegoat," but the *pharmakeus* is a "magician." The opposition of ideas held by single words and their derivatives tell us that there is no such thing as a harmless remedy, and that poisons will always have their redeeming features. The poison will always have within it the cure, and the cure will always hold within itself a complicity with the cause of the disease

Psychotherapy then cannot be taken primarily as a predominately "helping," "curing," or purely altruistic profession based on "understanding," though all those elements come into play. The action of therapy, or "attending to" the disorder of the patient, will always bring about a necessary pain of some kind for both patient and doctor. it is not until the doctor allows him/herself to be affected in some way by the distress of the patient that a resolution can come about in the patient. Jung writes, "It is the doctor's own hurt that gives the measure of his power to heal."[9] The myth of the wounded healer is telling us that countertransference is not just a form of awareness or consciousness to be developed, rather it is what brought the practitioner into the field and is always active in the analytic moment.

In conclusion, myth tells us that the psyche has a paradoxical self-healing tendency involving agencies beyond the will of the patient or doctor. Jung: "It is as though at the climax of the illness, the destructive powers were converted into healing forces."[10] Myth presents wounding as the ground of commonality between patient and doctor that gives rise to the healing nature of the bipolar, transference/countertransference dynamic. The question which brought about healing in the Grail legend, "whom does the Grail serve?" leads to the ethical question latent in every analytic moment: who and what is being served—patient, analyst, or the encompassing process of the work? What is the larger meaning of the encounter?. . .And the psyche provides entrances into this mythic mystery through the autonomous, inter-relationship of wounding/healing.

Out of Myth emerges Dream . . .

Endnotes

[1] Lindner, R., *The Fifty-Minute Hour*, pp. 204-5.

[2] Sedgwick, D., *The Wounded Healer*.

[3] Groesbeck, J., "The archetypal image of the wounded healer," Vol 20. No. 2, *The Journal of Analytical Psychology*, pp. 122-145.

[4] For the Navajo, the locust, a relative of the grasshopper, led the original people out of the underworld to the middle world of everyday existence.

[5] Kerenyi, K., *Asklepios: Archetypal Image of the Physician's Existence*, pp. 98-9.

[6] Malachi 4:2.

[7] Matthew 10: 34-36.

[8] In other versions, Sir Gauvain, another Grail hero who was knowledgeable in the use of medicinal herbs, sought out the bleeding lance and returned it to the king.

[9] Jung, C. G., *The Practice of Psychotherapy*, CW 16, pp. 98-9.

[10] Jung, *Psychology and Religion: West and East*, CW 11, p. 345.

Chapter Six

Gnostic Myth as Dream

Psychological Understanding

In *Memories, Dreams, Reflections,* Jung states, "I took great care to try to understand every single image, every item of my psychic inventory, and to classify them scientifically . . . and, above all, to realize them in actual life."[1] In attempting to establish the scientific validity of the unconscious, Jung was emphasizing the "other" as interior, i.e., images emerging from the unconscious. In *Psychology and Alchemy,* Jung writes, "The concept of *imaginatio* is perhaps the most important key to the understanding of the *opus.*"[2] Imagination, the "intermediate realm between mind and matter," is the "true expression" of the psyche. Psychological understanding of the "other," therefore, requires a "standing under," a significant sacrifice of assumptions, preconceptions, systems of comprehending, rational priorities, even of subjective identity, in order to encounter the "other" of the image and to address it on its (the work or *opus*) terms by "seeing through" to its core elements. Then the stage is set to live into the other, to experience it, to undergo it, to allow it to become an actual concrete presence as image within the psychic terrain.

Dreaming the Dream Onward

Dreams provide a space of virtual reality giving a perspective on the current internal psychological condition from the standpoint of the psyche's deepest perspective which most often runs counter to that of subjective consciousness. Dreams are not videos to be assessed objectively through concepts which kill off their contents, rather they are liminal worlds to be *entered into* and experienced through imagination. Dreams do not speak of the outer world and its circumstances and choices, rather they use external figures, behaviors, and situations, including the previous day's residues as context, to depict states of affairs through a logic of a different order than that of the rational ego. This depiction is often paradoxical relative to the ego's assumptions, in fact, turning these expectations upside down and uprooting the ego in an awakening to its actual dystonic being. Intimacy with repulsive figures are revealed as integration of concealed potential while heroic battling and overcoming of threatening figures and forces are indicative of ego defenses and resistance to assimilation. Every aspect and agent within the dream reveals itself as an internal object state, energy source or identity potential with an autonomous ground or life of its own, presenting itself to be experienced and explored such that *its* perspective and being can be lived into and experienced in conscious life. Dreams do not provide answers, prescriptions, directives for behavior or prophecies, rather they invite experience from which alternative ways of thinking and perceiving become possible, most often counter to the ego's perspectives and desires. The goal of dreams is to become an ongoing presence, always already available to the conscious psyche.

Dreaming the Myth

Dreams, as with all experience, are matters of perspective and therefore present themselves as both the subject and object of many ways of being, depending upon the particular lens used to engage them. We could say that as we read dreams, they also see us, read us, through a multitude of viewpoints. One lens, that of the mythic, seems particularly suited to dreams. Myth (*mythos*) means "story," but as we have seen it is etymologically associated with words of the unspoken—"mute," "mum," "mumble"—thereby enhancing our sensibility of the ultimately unknowable nature of dreams; they *have us*. Knowing the unknowable is the orientation of three great Middle Eastern religions—Judaism, Christianity, and Islam—all of which emerge from the underlying rhizome of mythic themes and images known in a general sense as gnosticism —gnosis meaning "knowledge," or more specifically, "knowledge of God."

Gnosticism provides a complex set of themes and images interrelated through a storyline regarding the emergence and differentiation of the soul through the coming to knowledge of a previously unknowable aspect of its nature. In a religious context, this part would be considered an element of the divine, whereas in a psychological sense, it would be considered the "unconscious," indications of which emerge through dreams. Like the dream, gnostic myth is a narrative, but one that is at once both linear and nonlinear, sequential and nonsequential, consisting of several nonhierarchic conditions that might be loosely differentiated as fallen world, descent, the call, the journey, the release, and a coming to knowledge. These stages are psychological *worlds* with associated feeling tones, action patterns, imagery, and consciousness, all governed by an archon or tutelary power; they are archetypal.

From the standpoint of gnostic myth, dreams can be seen as signifiers of specific psychological spaces, which, taken together, form a pattern of transformation or change. Associations to dreams tell us what these imaginal places look like in the everyday world of the dreamer's life. Furthermore, the act of dreaming itself can be considered a manifestation of one or more of these realms. The intention of this chapter is to delineate these worlds and to show how the content of dreams, as well as the act of dreaming, give them expression.

Fallen World

The gnostic universe originates divided and dualistic, without harmony, between two cosmic realms designated as the ideal and the mundane, knowledge and ignorance (*agnoia*), light and dark, heaven and earth, spirit and matter, above and below. The gnostic story takes place largely in the context of the "fallen world," the inferior aspect of any of these dyads, and moves toward an integration or "knowing" of the two worlds by each other.

The "fallen" realm is any psychological space that is consciously or unconsciously experienced as flawed or mistaken, disenchanted or disillusioned, stuck or imprisoned—eliciting depression, despair, and the feeling of death. It is a form of alchemical *nigredo* or darkness, in which processes of rotting, decomposing, decompensating, and wasting away dominate. The atmosphere is bitter, putrid, seedy, staid, stale, petrified. Fallen situations are expressed metaphorically as those that are decrepit, putrid, seedy and decaying. Fallen imagery includes structures that are falling apart, meetings never starting, dances not in step, stagnant parties, planes delayed and grounded. There is a pervasive sense that nothing works; everything is "just fucked."

Life situations reflecting the fallen world include relationships, gatherings, organizations, and performances that cannot get going or have gone on too long, operating under corrupted value systems or foundations, or going past the point of diminishing returns. There is a sense of things "going sour" or working against themselves, expressed in images conveying the "lost cause," where one is mired in quicksand, running on a treadmill or stuck on a sinking ship.

The lower world is bodily as opposed to spiritual, existing in the mode of sleep or forgetfulness or just plain drunk. The gnostic phrase "the noise of the world" refers to what we might consider "low life" or anything undesirable. No direction is known; no goal appears. In gnostic terms, one finds oneself a "stranger" or a "stranger in a strange land," or held "captive," "prisoner," "alien." The pervading feeling is one of homesickness, melancholia, nostalgia, and forlornness. The same old scenarios dominate, the same old song and dance prevails, and the same ol', same ol' remains the same.

"Rhonda," a writer/teacher married to an emotionally distant and highly defended husband, reported a dream which depicts the fallen world. She was severely abused as a child by her mother and therefore developed a deeply masochistic identity, now modified but not given up. Her writing is focused on giving voice to the "abused girl" through fictional narrative. She is in an affair with a geographically and psychologically distant man, D, who keeps her on a string through his seeming "understanding," which remains void of committed follow-through. She dreams the following:

> I am in D's house, exhausted after a long, arduous trip. I am in a small space. I hear arguing between D and his wife. I am too tired to deal with anything. D's wife comes in. She is a suburban-Botticellian beauty. She coldly looks through me as if I'm not there.

Rhonda's association to the dream is that it took place after her last analytic session, that dealt with the felt "unspeakability" of the abused girl in her novel and the hopeless feeling her writing takes on as "more debris" is injected into the world. In the dream, we can see the fallen world as a tired, masochistic realm of self-abuse and devaluation, where the dreamer goes unseen as the "ruined woman" by the harsh eye of conventional beauty as unattainable lovability she has taken in. This is a world she enters every time she writes, comes into her analytic sessions, or contacts her lover. Here the act of dreaming itself can be seen as an experience of a fallen condition, a discomforting dwelling below the surface of consciousness, away from the world of habitual, secure survival with its rounds of custom, practiced by the dreamer in her everyday mode of accommodation.

Descent

The lower, inferior world is attained through a fall, the purpose of which, in Jungian terms, is to achieve a more wholistic being by incorporating something of the psyche that has been kept separate and apart. An aspect of the soul in the upper realm becomes attracted to the lower world and a descent occurs—a sinking, a focus downward, the higher pulled to the lower, the pure into muck, where its sparks are scattered, the original dispersed into the derived. The experience is often one of darkness, defeat, or trauma, yet there is a necessity about it. In everyday life, words coming out of the head and put down on paper, or ideas submitted to the practical test of the world, take a "fall" from ideality into a more material, tangible state of being. "Falling in love" takes one out of a "purer" singular existence into the more complex condition of relationship. This falling condition comes in the form of physical falls, accidents, disappointments, natural disasters, losses in competitive endeavors, and through larger life losses such as job, relationship, or literal death of significant other. In analysis, an intervention or simply the flow of associations may "tip" the patient into a cluster of repressed thoughts or feelings such that defenses slip reluctantly away. The fall occurs in dreams through any kind of downward movement—down the escalator or elevator, the ladder, or the stairs, down the rabbit hole or off the cliff, dropping to lower levels of geography or buildings.

"Mona" is a single, professional woman in her late thirties, hungry for a committed relationship with a man with whom she could create a family. With her fortieth birthday looming, she is carrying a history of relationships, sulfurous in their quick, flaming quality, with "beautiful addicts"—charming men void of capacity for commitment. These relationships have been somewhat in reaction to her earlier enmeshment with an invasive, controlling, self-involved mother, so that her desire for these unavailable men comes with a hidden resistance of her own and a burden of responsibility. As a result, a doubly determined defense comes into play in her attraction to these men, the high of rapturous merging without the underlying threat of complex relationship.

In the midst of a budding new relationship, Mona had the following dream:

I am walking. My foot comes down in a mass of snakes—copperheads—that wrap around my foot but don't bite.

Her association to the dream was that the snakes, although poisonous, were not rattlers, like her image of mother. Gnostic myth might say that Mona is experiencing a fall into a complex of feelings (snakes) around: 1) a developing relationship that seems to be of a different quality than those of the past; 2) an obsessional attitude that includes mixed feelings (entanglement), newly renewed, toward finding relationship; and 3) the mother/daughter configuration, now revisited in a mediated mode (i.e., as copperheads, not rattlers). It can also be noted that copper, as a connector or conductor, is the metal of Aphrodite. The fact that the original *pharmakon* or healing herb was both a poison and a healer would give evidence that the patient's fall also pertains to a growing intimacy within the analytic relationship. From a gnostic point of view, dreaming itself can be seen as an act of falling—that is, falling from a comfortable, rational mode of the dayworld into the relative discomfort of the irrational, confusing, "inferiority" of the nightworld of images and feelings that comprise the dream experience.

Call from Without

In gnostic myth the invisible counterpart of the lost soul embedded in the fallen world— that is, the spiritual "other"—at some point, develops a yearning for its imprisoned or forgotten aspect and sends an emissary or Redeemer to correct the situation. This second descent is in service to a "retrieval" that involves a taking on of the "clothes of the world" by the messenger. The emissary appears to the lost soul and declares a revelation, a message of re-minding or re-membering: Greetings, Ave Maria! Awake, you drowsy sleeper! Become alive to your true being! The existence you are experiencing is inauthentic and temporary. Your condition is alien to the spiritual nature of your real self. You belong in a different place. Get back to where you once belonged! Return to your origins—come home! Realize your true path!"

The "call" can be thought of as any indicator pointing to a need for change, usually accompanied by a feeling of discomfort. The change can be in identity, lifestyle, or stage in life. The call may emerge via a pull for regression, issued within an old way of being, now dysfunctional, and resulting in feelings of depression or yearning. The call can be an actual verbal communication, a physical or mental breakdown or dysfunction, an unusual loss of control such as an emotional outburst, or a material catastrophe such as an auto accident or house burning down. From the gnostic perspective, anything in psychotherapy regarded as a "symptom" could be seen as a call from the unconscious indicating that change is needed or is taking place according to the psyche's system of self-healing. Dreams of dark figures or of animals approaching or following the dreamer or trying to get into the dreamer's dwelling are manifestations of the call for change that is already underway.

As a child "Bill" was sexually, physically, and emotionally abused by various family members, including his domineering stepfather, R,. Depressed and lonely, Bill wants a family of his own yet relates to women in a style of emotional domination that compensates for his low self-esteem. He is working to separate himself from stringent family connections, literal and psychological, and dreams the following:

> I get a phone *call* from my mother and sister to meet them with R. I am waiting at the airport gate for them. Their flight is delayed until the next night. I go back to my hotel. Next night, no arrival. It turns out they had arrived at the next gate, No. 28, two or three hours ago. I text my sister. They are staying with a friend of theirs. I drive there and ring the doorbell. My sister answers in a matter-of-fact way. R walks over. He is a shell of a person, hunched and shaking, incoherent. I barely hear him mutter, "I love you," but the life force is gone from him. My sister gives me a look as if to make me feel guilty, but I don't. She comments how treatments to restore R actually are killing him and she is his caretaker.

Bill's association to the dream was that R was now lifeless, similar to the way he feels in his own life. The call is bringing attention to a change that is occurring in Bill: His will to dominate is dying away through "treatment." The call also is from a guilt (sister) that resists the psychoanalysis ("treatment") that is working upon the domination—inferiority complex represented in R. What is treatment to one part of the psyche is poison to another.

Later, Bill has another dream.:

I am at my place, putting on a dinner party for three. Good time being had by all. Doorbell *rings*. I answer and it is M, my maternal grandmother.

Bill responded to this dream with the realization that in years of analytic work, he had forgotten about M and had left her out of his thinking related to family. He said, "She died when I was seventeen, but was the only family member I was ever close to. She hated the other (abusive) members of the family; I could just tell. She read me stories and saw me as special." In the gnostic orientation, the emissary from beyond becomes a helper or guide to provide instruction. In the dream a self-affirming guide has appeared from within at a very dark time to influence Bill's identity in the world as a unique being whose presence is wanted. "Now I can show up!" he exclaimed, referring to his sense of self in relationship and work.

Within the gnostic framework, dreams act as the call, in and of themselves. Dreams are the animals and the unknown figures representing a new element to be included in the dreamer's personality, the harbingers of a more encompassing being.

Journey

The theme of the return involves a journey of homecoming, not a return to a false condition, but to a re-newed or re-membered essential condition that has been left behind. For the gnostic, the present state is only a sojourn; a journey of transformation is required. The journey is one of travail, involving a wandering through the unredeemed world, often imaged as following a meandering trail, gathering lost or forgotten "sparks" or aspects of the soul. The journey need not be one of space or time, nor representative of stages of transformation. Rather, it is a process of assimilation or integration of that which is seen from a more limited, mundane perspective as "other." Psychologically speaking, dreams are journeys that include occasions for integration through the appearances or epiphanies of characters or creatures representing different worlds or ways of being that are repugnant to the dreamer's conscious values, but latent in the dreamer's unconscious.

Consider "Dolores," who is struggling with a conflict in identity between being a dependent, compliant daughter aligned with the values of her patriarchal foreign culture and a cosmopolitan woman of the world. She dreams:

> I am at my house in this country. The house has a floor like that in my home country. A family member lets in a blind woman beggar from the backyard while I am in my room. I come out and see the woman finding her way around the house to beg. I am angry that she was let in. She is so intrusive! She finds me and begs. I say, "No," and kick her out. Then I feel guilty. My son may be harmed because of my action.

The patient's associations to the dream were that in her culture, the belief is that rejecting a beggar brings harm. The blind woman reminded Dolores of a certain woman in her community whom she was avoiding because this woman presumed to take a stance as mother to her. Applying a gnostic sensibility, the patient is being confronted with a "poor, blind" neediness in herself that invites mothering and that she needs to integrate in order to attain her psychological journey's destination of authenticity as a woman.

Another example: "Kristin" brings in a poem as a gift to her analyst, only to be traumatized by the analyst's spontaneous interpretive response. She dreams:

> I am with my grandson (age 8) in the backyard. There is a hole in the ground. A huge snakehead appears. I am terrified.

From the gnostic perspective, the snake as serpent would represent a primal force essential to her core being, evoked by a transference-countertransference enactment that took her to the place of a child. Historically, the event corresponded to her own childhood experience of being "dissed" by her mother. The subsequent working through her feelings and integration of the snake energy would allow Kristin to make a movement away from a dependent position with the analyst and in her life.

Dreams are the journey in that they take the dreamer on a trip into a different world with a seemingly unintelligible logic and an unfamiliar set of underlying assumptions, inhabited by strange subjects. The dream is an underworld to the dayworld which forms his or her customary but limited identity—all of which can be "taken in" to form a new perspective from a once foreign territory.

Release

During the gnostic journey of transformation, a time comes when will and conscious intentionality give out. At this point of necessary surrender, a larger, autonomous force can take over and carry the process in conjunction with the exhausted will. The giving over of conscious intention allows for receptivity to the otherness of the soul that the weary traveler is destined to incorporate.

"Sonia" is struggling with the lifelong sense of always needing to organize herself around the values and expectations of others. This driving need stems historically from her unconscious need to be of value to her father. The struggle has often resulted in her defensive, countermove of resistance to others in a position of authority. At an annual business conference at which she had normally found herself skeptical and on-guard, she had a series of dreams:

> I dreamed of a young boy in my care. He had removed his own kidneys to present to CS, who I think was his mother. It was all very "clean," not bloody; they [the kidneys] looked a bit like living jewels.

Her association to kidneys was that their function is to screen out toxins, and that her father had had his kidneys removed as the first site of his cancer. "CS" is an old friend with whom she

101

has been out of touch for years, a misfit who easily discounted others, who tried hard as if she had something to prove, who was self-deprecating, and who got by, slipping in "under the wire." These are all qualities which had previously resonated in Sonia herself, and we can imagine that she was letting go of a screening defense of skepticism which would open her to the unformed aspect of her self-image as depicted in a subsequent dream.

Days earlier Sonia had dreamed of a plane being unable to successfully take off and being forced to come to a hard landing. A female passenger, who was associated with a woman who didn't get "pulled off her path by others," was catapulted into the row ahead of Sonia and straddled another seated passenger, face to face, as if a "descent" and "fall" had resulted in an erotic encounter resulting in something other than steadfast resilience. Here, Sonia is presented with the potential (one row ahead) of another part in herself representing self-empowerment.

Sonia's dream three:

There is a mother, a father, and a child in the dream (not me or my parents). The child is somehow connected to electricity from a wall socket, which keeps the child attached and unable to move away. Both the mother and the father try to pull the child away from the electricity. Neither of them is impacted by it, but their efforts are in vain. Finally, the father frees the child, takes it outside and releases it, like you would release a balloon, and it disappears. I also sense the child being a duplex figure, like it is a child and a frog or toad, at the point where the father releases it.

Sonia's associations were that electricity was a form of energy and that a frog was a "caring," amphibious creature at home in two elements. A gnostic understanding of this dream would see a "release" from that which the child had been heretofore "plugged into" as a central source of energy. Release was brought about by the inner character, representing father/authority/analyst, indicating a new relationship to this figure. (These dreams were the first in several years of analysis that were typed and given to the analyst.) Letting go also marks the place of a crucial connection to amphibious or instinctual nature. In a larger sense, dreaming itself is a way of letting go of rational consciousness and will, "letting it all hang out," providing for the experience of release that leads to an ultimate integration of "knowledge."

Knowledge

In gnostic mythology, the journey of transformation through the realization of knowledge via an encounter with representatives of the "other" culminates in the ultimate meeting with the unknowable counterpart. Psychologically, apotheosis consists in the soul redeeming itself by meeting its unknown aspect, now "knowing" itself as if for the first time. The redemption is one of knower and known in complete sympathy with each other through a unique, essential state signified by harmonious alignment.

Sonia had the following dream, subsequent to those in the "release" realm:

There are four groups of horses; each group is forming a circle. The horses remind me of Lipizzaners. They are moving into a precise position in each circle. There is one circle that I have an especially clear view of. I have a sense of the last horse in that circle settling into position. At that moment I felt a shudder run through the middle of my body (horizontally) and I woke up.

A shudder is the archetypal bodily sensation that signals an encounter with an encompassing or "larger than" entity. In mythology, encounters with gods are often accompanied by a shudder on the part of the mortal (Leda and the swan). Sonia has come to feel that she is "of value" regardless of whether "father" ("other" as authority) knows she knows and whether she has sufficiently prepared to prove herself "ready." Her elegant, performative horsepower (Lipizzaner breed of show horse) has come into alignment; she now is the readiness itself.

"Don," a young man in the middle of a prolonged identity crisis, dreams the following as he is coming to realize what his lifework will be:

I am by a pool in the forest. It looks inviting, and I go swimming. While in the pool I notice there is a snake in each of the four corners. I quickly get out. As I stand up on shore and look back into the water, the snakes converge at one end of the pool. They are joined by a fifth snake with four tails in the shape of a lute or some kind of musical instrument or notation. The snakes form a straight line and swim across the pool in formation.

Ironically, the analysis of this man is still a "long way from home," with the journey of self-discovery having just gotten underway, but the dream gives a premonition of getting there. The snakes represent primal energies that are finding their way into alignment. The dreamer can connect to this energy only when he gains a reflective perspective.

The function of apotheosis works through dreams as such, in that dreams act as a mirror image of the "other"—the unknowable sides of ourselves through which our unique sense of being may be experienced in its fullness. The gnostic cycle is never completed, different fundamental conditions do not necessarily occur in any chronological order and dreams do not mark a lasting change. The psyche, as fundamentally hermetic, works in elliptical cycles, always coming round again to the point from which it started, but a little different each time around. In addition, dreams need to be considered within the context of the associations they elicit and the immediate everyday context that the psyche is taking into account through the dream. In the interplay of the dream with these various elements related to the dream, a web may be woven, decipherable through a gnostic orientation, giving an image of the sacred within the mundane of everyday life.

Out of Dream emerges Mirror . . .

Endnotes

[1] Jung, C. G., *Memories, Dreams, Reflections*, p. 192.
[2] Jung, *Psychology and Alchemy* CW 12, p. 279.

Chapter Seven

Self/Other: The Infinite Wilderness of Mirrors

"I celebrate myself, and sing myself,
And what I assume you shall assume,
For every atom belonging to me as good belongs to you."
                                        -Walt Whitman, "Leaves of Grass"

"Jill and Jack both want to be wanted.

Jill wants Jack because he wants to be wanted
 Jack wants Jill because she wants to be wanted.

Jill wants Jack to want
  *Jill to want
          Jack's want of her want
               for his want of
                    her to want Jack to want*

*repeat sine fine"
                                        -R. D. Laing, *Knots*

"For now we see through a glass darkly; but then face to
face: now I know in part; but then shall I know even as
also I am known."
                                        -I Corinthians 13:12

"In a wilderness of mirrors. What will the spider do...?"
                                        -T.S. Eliot, "Gerontion"

In the healing practices of many native peoples, a breakdown in individual relationship with community can be the cause of dysfunction and the involvement of community in the ceremonies is essential for healing to be effective. This factor in healing reveals a fundamental ontology, namely the psychological interface of self and other through the integral relation of self and community. In the case of the Navajo, members of the community enact ceremonial roles and the entire community helps in the preparation of rituals. In turn, the healing that occurs in the individual is a healing of community as well. For the Cochiti pueblo in New Mexico, individual malaise is caused by wrong relationship to clan. Healing ceremonies involve initiatory rites in which the individual is adopted by a clan. The Ndembu in Africa consider attunement and adherence to an extremely complex system of social roles, lineage and hierarchy as determinant of individual well-being. Healing consists of a series of rites partaken by the community, bringing the individual into proper social alignment and subsequent healing. The Ubuntu consider the individual to become human through relationship to others and the dehumanization of others as the simultaneous dehumanization of self. Jung wrote ". . . relationship to the self is at once relationship to our fellow man . . . Individuation . . . is an . . . indispensable process of objective relationship."[1]

This chapter is about an idea: what we think of as "self" is *created* in conjunction with an *other*. It takes an other for me to be me. I am who I am in combination with the who with whom I am. My "self" is an event that takes place within a context. "I borrow myself from others."[2] The idea has two aspects: identity is a matter of making; it is a work in progress. The process of self-creation is always a co-creation; we are always co-constituted with an other, our story always co-authored, the self always fluid, an in-between phenomenon. A patient whose mother could only look at him with rage demands of his analyst, "Where is your hatred of me? I need it so that I can take it in and exist with you." Another patient described his life at home as being constantly created through his fantasy of his wife's varying attitudes towards him. On the other hand, when he was alone in a mountain vacation home, he imagined an eye on him to be the warmth of the enfolding pines, and he could relax.

What is meant by "other?" Other, is on one hand, a literal experience—How do I fit into the literal environment of people and things? Who am I in relation to the person sitting across from me, coming toward me, walking beside me? What is the life of the actual space which I inhabit? And, it is an imaginal or "as if" experience of representations—the persons or things which make up my internal context signify something to me, an eye watching, a voice speaking. The "other" is, on the one hand, anything that is in some sense separate, conjuring a feeling of anxiety that comes with a sense of my particularity. In the 16th century, Montaigne wrote, "Likeness does not make things 'one' so much as unlikeness makes them 'other.'"[3] I become unique to myself as an other appears in my world. At the same time, the other refers to an enveloping image, scene or drama in which I have a part, a matrix or medium from which my I-ness emerges regardless of external context. Our "being" then is always a matter of dialogue within a context in which we are separate from or part of, revealed as both literal and imaginal.

In the film "Cast Away," the main character finds himself stranded alone on an island with some of the cargo from a Federal Express plane on which he had been travelling before it crashed. By accident, he places his bloodied hand on a Wilson volleyball and notices that the imprint forms a face. The head that has been formed by the ball becomes his companion, "Wilson," with whom he confides his deepest thoughts and feelings.[4] This image of face as implanted blood indicates the dynamic of the creation of "other" as that which carries our suffering. The character becomes so attached to Wilson that when he leaves the island on a precarious journey, he takes Wilson with him and is distraught when the ball accidentally rolls overboard and floats away. The eye of a passing whale serves for a moment as other, and the character is finally rescued when "seen" by a passing ship.

In his autobiography, C. G. Jung, who often found himself alone as a boy, describes two ways in which he created an "other."

He would sit on a rock and ask, "Am I the boy sitting on the rock or the rock imagining the boy?" He also carved a figure of a little man, placed it in a pencil box and hid it in the attic so that he could converse with it as his "inner self" whenever and wherever he felt the need. It is as if we are always "pursuing" a self by "aiming" ourselves at the world, and the road to an inner sense of self always passes through a created external other. The created "self" uses the autonomous life, the subjectivity of the "other" and its desires, to form its own "being." When we are, we are always in the condition of that which sees an other seeing us upon whom we are always "co-dependent."

The Play's the Thing

The ontology, or sense of being of self through an other, is well illustrated in existential French theatre. The French playwright, Jean Genet, was abandoned by his mother at an early age and raised by poor foster parents in Paris. He spent a great deal of time in the streets, and at an early age he was accused of stealing and prostitution. He resolved at that point to be as he was seen by the world.

> "Abandoned by my family, I found it natural to aggravate this fact by the love of males, and that love by stealing, and stealing by crime, or the complicity with crime. Thus I decisively repudiated a world that had repudiated me."[5]

Genet is saying that society needs the thief and the prostitute, like the master needs a slave or the perpetrator, the victim, and all vice versa. He would find his identity in the subsidiary role. The society sets up the crime; the thief and prostitute commit it.

Genet led his adolescent life as an itinerant juvenile delinquent, involved in thieving and prostitution, living in and out of prisons all over Europe. Eventually, he came across Stilitano, a tall, handsome, one-handed Serbian pimp who became a hero and model for Genet. One day, Stilitano and Genet went to a fair. They came across a hall of mirrors, a labyrinth of reflections in which one would enter and then try to get out, all the while being observed by the crowd outside. Stilitano went in and became confused by the mirror images. He got lost and couldn't get out while the crowd outside bore witness and laughed at the spectacle of his struggle.

"Stilitano was alone. Everyone had found the way out except him. Strangely, the universe veiled itself for me. The shadow that suddenly fell over things and people was the shadow of my solitude confronted with this despair, for, no longer able to shout, to butt himself against the walls of glass, resigned at being a mockery for the gaping crowd, Stilitano had crouched down on the floor, refusing to go on."[6]

While the sense of being trapped in a hall of mirrors may be a fitting image of the experience of psychotherapy and the many selves of patient and therapist reflecting each other, Genet used the image of the human trapped like an animal in a maze of reflected self-images co-created by the subject and others as a dominant theme in his plays. In his first play, "Deathwatch," three prisoners are in a cell, indicating life as imprisonment by other people. Green Eyes is a tough guy, the dominant one in the group. He has been convicted of murder and is due to be executed. Maurice, a younger man, adores Green Eyes. LeFranc also wants Green Eyes' attention and is jealous of Maurice, whom he taunts as being weak. A hierarchical power structure is set up in which the submissive need the dominant as much as the dominant need the submissive. It is also a circular configuration of mirrors enacted by an other for each of the three individual selves. Green Eyes needs the adoration of Maurice to maintain an identity as dominant. Maurice needs the acknowledgement of LeFranc to maintain a sense of adequacy. LeFranc needs the recognition of Green Eyes for his feeling of power.

The dramatic action occurs with the cracking of each of the three mirroring objects. Green Eyes breaks down in telling the story of his crime, the killing of a mere prostitute in blind rage, and loses his heroic image for Maurice. Le Franc strangles Maurice, depriving Green Eyes of Maurice's adulation. Green Eyes, not needing LeFranc since he has received recognition through a gift of cigarettes from Snow Ball, an unseen convict even higher in the prison hierarchy, refuses to acknowledge LeFranc's manhood. The play ends with LeFranc's realization "I am alone." For Genet, when the mirrors of illusion, which we create through others, break, what is left is an abyss of darkness, alienation, emptiness, fear, and despair. The question remains, can we ever leave the hall of mirrors, or is our existence always created through a set of illusions?

In Genet's play, "The Maids," two women are seen in an 18th century bedroom: an elegant "Madame" being dressed by her maid, "Claire." The two taunt each other as the "Madame" is quite haughty, and eventually she is slapped by the maid. An alarm rings and the scene collapses. The two women are then revealed to be both sisters and maids, enacting the relationship between maid and Madame. "Claire" is not Claire at all, but Solange who had been acting the maid, "Claire," while the maid named Claire had played the part of the "Madame."

In other words, a three-tiered mirror is being enacted at the theatre event—actress, playing maid, playing either "Madame" or "maid"—with the implication that the chain of mirrors goes on forever. Only when they are being "false," playing the role of the "other," can their true feelings be revealed. When Claire as "Madame" tells Solange as "Claire," "Keep your hands off mine! I can't stand you touching me," she is speaking as both the Madame to the maid and sister to sister. The literal slap of the Madame by Solange as "Claire" the maid, is the first breaking of a "whirligig" of mirror of identities.

The two maids are bound to each other and to the Madame by affection; playing the role of the other is an act of desire, and a deep hatred, the enactment of ritual denigration. When the Madame is out, they enact a fantasy of alternating servility (love) and revolt (hatred) leading to her death, which is left unaccomplished, always in potential. In other words, as with any intimate relationship, the ties of love are bound by hatred engendered when the other turns out not to be the character into which the subject is attempting to make them. Claire declares to Solange, "I'm sick of seeing my image thrown back at me by a mirror, like a bad smell. You're my bad smell." We identify ourselves through the repugnant odor of the other, needing the hatred as much as the loving of the other.

The two maids have plotted to have the Madame's lover jailed, but when he is released, they panic, and plot to kill the Madame by poisoning her tea. Their scheming is again foiled when the Madame finds out about her lover's release and rushes off to find him. The two maids resume the game of maid and "Madame," only this time Claire plays the role of the Madame to its ultimate authenticity and drinks the cup of poisonous tea. The ritual abuse, or murder of the loved and envied object, repeated over and over, has reached its climax, and the mirror is shattered one last time. The self-certain "I" through which we observe the world and organize our experience is itself a mirror and collapses, leaving void, despair, and the desperate necessity of another maize of mirrors in the carnival of psychic life.

Genet's play, "The Balcony," takes place in a brothel, where customers come and take on the role of bishop, judge, general, and Foreign Legionnaire—all served by whores in appropriately complementary roles. Again, the metaphor is telling; we are all whores to each other. The only one not playing a role is the Police Chief, who knows that only when someone comes in asking to play his role, will he have power. A revolution is going on and the leader of the revolutionaries, Roger, comes in asking to be the Police Chief. In playing the role of Police Chief, he castrates himself, breaking the mirror by simultaneously punishing himself for his desire for power and the "Police Chief" for having power. Just as with Claire poisoning herself in the role of "the Madame," self-destruction is revealed as co-constituted by both the subject and the supposed object of the aggression.

Jean Paul Sartre, the French existential philosopher and Genet's contemporary, wrote an essay, "St. Genet," suggesting that Genet's claim to sainthood lay in the absolute authenticity with which he accepted the relativity of his condition. Sartre also wrote a play, "No Exit," which reflects the themes in Genet's work. In the play, three characters are in a single room: Garcin, a coward who proclaims himself a pacifist, but who in fact, deserted his friends and was shot by a firing squad, Inez, a cynical lesbian, who was killed by her lover, and Estelle, a vain woman of supposedly high taste, who was in fact, a mistress who killed her own baby. There is no window or mirror in the room, again suggesting that it is people who serve as windows and mirrors for each other. This conceit unfolds during the play in which the relationship among the three is developed. The underlying question that drives the play is: "Why are the three of us together?"

Garcin looks to Estelle for confirmation of his manhood, but Inez casts doubt on anything Estelle might say by taunting Garcin with the fact that Estelle will do anything to get the eye of a man, leaving Garcin in need of acknowledgement of Inez. Estelle, the murderer of her own child (she can't stand the reflection of herself in the baby,) needs Garcin to mirror her beauty back to her. Inez needs Estelle's love and offers her love as a means through which Estelle might love herself. Each character needs the eyes of one of the others to reflect him or herself.

Estelle is afraid of what she might see of herself and her inability to tame the image of herself through Inez's eyes and therefore looks to Garcin, the man, for whom she would represent beauty. Inez, needing Estelle, won't let her be seen by Garcin, reminding him that Estelle will do anything to get the eye of a man. Garcin, in turn, must look to Inez for validation, but she is only capable of seeing him as a coward. Each is then left with the task of creating a mirror of self in the eye of one who is unwilling to reflect that image. The task is so compelling, none of the three can leave when the door is open. They realize they are in hell, as if life itself is a place of limbo, a perpetual subjugation to the co-created torture of human relationship.

Sartre, in his seminal work, *Being and Nothingness*, wrote that being itself is a matter of the reciprocal action of seeing and being seen which lends itself to a changing identity. "I *am* as the

Other sees me . . . he has established me in a new type of being which can support new qualifications."[7] Our interior sense of self is accomplished through a reciprocal dynamic with the external. I am only as I am organized through the other. An other is the truth of me, as I am the truth of the other. The approach and presence of the other is at the same time the approach and presence of myself. This fluid sense of identity has its own intentionality, its own direction of flow. I am aimed, leaning toward an other as if haunting the world in my perpetual pursuit of self through other.

The other is not the literal person in my gaze, rather the person represents a "larger than," transcendental realm, a world of associated, multiple and experiential meanings. The other is an image, a phantom,[8] The other is more than just a human being; it consists of the things of the world in my environment, each of which has its own hidden subjectivity that sees me or talks to me. Each thing or milieu, as other, has its own eye or voice concealed in the surface or if, a person, *behind* the literal eyes and voice perceived. The world of people and things then becomes that through which I become and am known to myself and others.

We are entertaining the idea that alone or with another, we are always "in-formed" by an other through dialogue. Paradoxically, we can only "know thyself" through the context of an other. I am who I am in conjunction with others; I am self and other at once. I know the self I am through the reflection of an other, just as I know the other through a reflection of self. Further, I become as I am aware of an other's reflection of me, and as I become more of an other to another self. Self and other are mutually and simultaneously interpenetrating and receiving of each other in a constant spiraling flow or flux. We live always already as borderline personalities on the edge between inner and outer, codependent and multiple in personality. From Genet's and Sartre's sensibility, we gather the idea that identity is formulated through images created in part by others—images which sooner or later are destroyed, leaving "self" in a condition that existentialists called "nothingness," but which can also lead on to a furthering of the self-as-image-building process. Identity formation can be seen as a dependent personality, sensing itself through sniffing out others via imagination.

The dynamic of alternating creation/destruction of identity through inter-relationship with another is especially poignant in the psychoanalytic field. When the creation breaks, the mirror cracking, the individual is left to experience a "re-visioning" process which for some turns into a psychotherapeutic relationship in which the inevitable ruptures can be experienced and explored. The therapist with attunement to the patient's consciousness, experiences herself as within the rupturing process. The patient needs to create therapist into a certain role, and the therapist needs to be able to hold that role no matter how painfully distant it is from the therapist's self-perception. The patient will make the therapeutic relationship a kind of prison, make believe show, brothel, or room of "no exit" that the therapist experiences as well. Within this space, the patient will paint the therapist with the blood-stained hand of suffering into the dominator or subordinate object, the Madame or the servant, the whore or the customer, the desired or the desiring one, the perfume or the stench of their own hidden being. The therapist, in turn, will co-create the scene, becoming the complementary figure to the patient out of the therapist's own experience. This dynamic holds until it's inevitable destruction that then leads to another bi-polar relational dynamic, potentially more in alignment with the patient's and therapist's more actual capacities and limitations.

The Purloined Letter

Our discussion of the inter-subjectival formulation of self/other in the bipolar psychotherapeutic field as anticipated in literature inevitably takes us to the 19th century American writer, Edgar Allen Poe, who prefigured psychodynamic psychotherapy in many ways. Poe wrote "horror stories," which from a psychological standpoint, could be seen as expressions of repressed beating of the "telltale heart" of unconscious contents. He wrote detective stories, which anticipated the analytic mode of therapy, finding the unknown cause of symptoms by following a trail of clues, analysis in service to the "hermeneutics of suspicion." His use of language was one of giving voice to unseen and unknown entities making themselves known, voices that are trapped, calling, or persecuting.

The French psychoanalyst, Jacques Lacan, points us to a story by Edgar Allen Poe that illustrates the multiple mirroring phenomena of the psychotherapeutic situation:[9]

> The Queen is alone in her boudoir with a letter. The King enters. The Queen wishes to conceal the letter and lays it on the table. The King doesn't see this gesture, and the Queen sees him not seeing. The Minister enters, sees the letter and recognizes the handwriting. The Queen sees him seeing and recognizing the letter and, knowing him to be without scruples, is concerned. The Minister sees her seeing his seeing of the letter and resulting consternation and, knowing the Queen perceives him to be without scruples, fathoms her secret regarding the letter. The Minister engages in conversation during which he pulls out a letter like the one in question, reads it out loud as if part of the conversation, and lays it down beside the Queen's letter. He converses further, then picking up the Queen's letter as if it were his own, places it in his pocket and leaves, all the while seeing the Queen see his actions. The Minister now has power over the Queen.
>
> The Queen employs the Prefect (police official) to retrieve the letter. The Prefect uses all the latest techniques of detection, but is unable to find the letter, and the Minister sees his not seeing. The Prefect comes to the detective, Dupin, and tells his story. Dupin sees that the Prefect can't see and that the Minister sees the Prefect not seeing. Dupin goes to the Minister's apartment under a pretext, sees the letter in a most obvious place (turned inside out, resealed, and placed

in an open letter holder), and returns it to the Prefect who returns it to the Queen.

The story posits three separate but related subjective positions, which are inter-subjectival in that the positions are what they are in relationship to the other two.

1) Subject is "blind," sees nothing. In the first tableau, this position is held by the King.

2) Subject "sees" first subject's blindness and takes advantage but is unaware of being seen. This position is first held by the Queen.

3) Subject as "robber" sees the other two subjects and procures the secret. This position is taken in the first case by the Minister.

In the second scene, the roles stay the same, but the characters shift. Now, the Queen is "blind" in that the Prefect, in her stead, cannot find the letter. The second position is now taken by the Minister, who sees the Queen's blindness, but doesn't see himself being seen by Dupin. The third position is taken by Dupin, who sees the other two and becomes the "robber" at the expense of the "seer." Identity here is determined in an inter-subjectival manner, not from an internal essence, but by the position in relation to other subjectivities.

We see this happening in therapeutic situations when the therapist is presented with a situation where the patient harbors that which is "secret" to his or her consciousness, which makes itself known through a symptom. If we follow Lacan and pose this therapeutic situation as analogous to Poe's story, then we might have a configuration as follows: the patient is in the first position, not seeing the unconscious cause of his or her pain. This "secret" would be analogous to the letter. The symptom (depression, anxiety, etc.) might be seen as a subjectivity that holds the secret (desire), sees the patient's blindness to the secret, but does not see the therapist seeing it, the symptom. The therapist would then be in the third position seeing both the patient's blindness and the symptom's seeing of the patient while holding the secret, but not seeing the therapist's seeing of it, the symptom. The therapist "robs" the symptom by revealing the secret through an interpretation, suggestion or reflection.

The therapist, in turn, runs the danger of being the subject in the first position, blind to his or her own desires in relation to the patient (second position,) which then get expressed in an "enactment" such as responding to the patient with a self-gratifying intervention or breaking the analytic container in some manner such that the third position is then awaited in the form of the therapist's renewed consciousness of his/her own unconscious needs.

I and Thou regarding I and Thou

Sartre presents the dark side of the self/other configuration, but he also states that "God appears as the quintessence of the Other."[10] In contrast to the existentialist perspective of the hellish nature of the inevitable interrelation of self with other, is that of the Hassidic philosopher, Martin Buber. Buber distinguishes between an objectified connection between people or between people and things, "I-It," and a relatedness of one's "whole being," "I-You." Likewise, Jung noted the resistance of the psyche to being objectified when he said, "...nothing is more unbearable to the patient than to be always understood."[11] In his concept of I-You, Buber brought the traditional Hebraic relationship of man and God to earth. God can only be spoken to in the present, "Jahweh" meaning "He is present." From this perspective, when one perceives and accepts another in the other's full being, as uncomfortable and with the loss of control as that might leave one, God is present. "When I confront a human being as my You . . . everything lives in his light."[12] Relationship in its immediacy, acts as a vehicle for the ancient Jewish theme of returning to God. Buber brings God to earth through authentic relationship.

The "I"-"You" relationship dissolves boundaries of subject and object, providing an emergent unity. "Where You is said there is no something. You has no borders."[13] It eliminates all notions of possession. "Whoever says You does not have something; he has nothing. But he stands in relation."[14] "Relation," for Buber, stands in opposition to a concept "causality," which has more to do with the subject-object quality of the "I"-"It" connection. "As long as the firmament of the You is spread over me, the tempests of causality cower at my heels, and the whirl of doom congeals."[15] In other words, there is no mediator in my relation to "You." No preconception intervenes, no prior knowledge, no bias, no expectations. "Only where all means have disintegrated encounters occur."[16]

As "I"-"You" is a manifestation of God, it occurs not by striving for it, but through grace. We can't try for this kind of relationship; we can only develop an ability to be available to it when it happens. "You" encounters me; I elect to engage with you. In engaging with you, I let go of my sense of volition, my sense of myself, and in doing so, come into the truth of my own being. This formation of identity is like the creation of a work of art. Just as the work of art requires an artist to bring it into being, "I require a You to become; becoming I, I say You."[17] Or we might also say we require an other as midwife to birth a self through becoming. What we call development of identity or personality is becoming and becoming is returning—returning to God but also returning to origins. "Every developing human child rests, like all developing beings in the womb of the great mother—the undifferentiated, not yet formed primal world."[18] Development then takes on a cyclical rather than linear quality. "Man becomes an I through a You. What confronts us comes and vanishes, relational events take shape and scatter, and through these changes crystallizes, more and more each time, the consciousness of the constant partner, the I-consciousness."[19]

Being in "I"-"You" means that life becomes an encounter or that one encounters Being. "Encounter" gives an uncomfortable, unreliable quality to Being because all ability to control the situation or "authorize" the story is removed. Being has its own autonomy.

"The world that appears to you in this way is unreliable, for it appears always new to you, and you cannot take it by its word. It lacks density, for everything in it permeates everything else. It lacks duration, for it comes even when not called and vanishes even when you cling to it. It cannot be surveyed: if you try to make it surveyable, you lose it. It comes—comes to fetch you—and if it does not reach you or encounter you it vanishes, but it comes again, transformed."[20]

"I"-"You" comes with grace and goes on its own accord leaving its indelible impression. Between you and it there is a reciprocity of giving:

". . . you say You to it and give yourself to it; it says You to you and gives itself to you. You cannot come to an understanding about it with others; you are lonely with it; but it teaches you to encounter others and to stand your ground in such encounters; and through the grace of its advents and the melancholy of its departures it leads you to that You in which the lines of relation, though parallel, intersect. It does not help you to survive; it only helps you to have intimations of eternity."[21]

"I"-"You," finally, as ideal model reinforces the sense of self/other consciousness in the uncertainty of a "larger than" space which is encompassed by the bi-polar field of psychoanalysis.

Psyche as Mirror

The French word for a free-standing, full length mirror is *psyche*, and throughout human history the mirror has served as a symbol of psychological self-reflection.[22] The shiny surface as an "other," which reflects the image of man, has been in existence since antiquity when glass-like stones, pools of water and shields were depicted as acting like mirrors. The Greeks used polished metal attached to a handle as a literal mirror and later the Romans used obsidian. The glass mirror was invented in Sidon around 3 A. D. Metal was used for mirrors in European countries until the 17th century when glass blowing enabled the glass mirror to be manufactured, followed by the silvered glass mirror we know today. In Greek mythology, the best-known reflected self-image is that of Narcissus in the pond, but Perseus' use of the shield to defeat Medusa with her image also gives evidence of the power of the reflection literalized.

The sense of the therapist acting as mirror for the patient begins with Plato. For Plato, the mirror reflection was an essential aspect for "care of the soul." The soul needs its image reflected in order to "see" its essence or to "know" itself. The image closest to truth is presented by the lover, thus the mirror image is a deception, but one which allows for the contemplation of essence. The mirror served as a signifier of a signifier or a mediator in a chain of hierarchical signifiers. The soul's journey to knowledge begins with the physical body and the lover's desire for the gaze of the other.

> "...(T)he flood of passion pours in upon the lover. And part of it is absorbed within him, and as a breath of wind or an echo, rebounding from a smooth hard surface, goes back to its place of origin even so the stream of beauty turns back and reenters the eyes of the fair beloved. And so by the natural channel it reaches his soul and gives it fresh vigor, watering the roots of the wings and quickening them to growth . . . So he loves, yet knows not what he loves . . . he cannot account for it, not realizing that his lover is, as it were, a mirror in which he beholds himself."[23]

Here the transference/countertransference relationship is beautifully anticipated as one in which the lover's soul, the soul of the patient, is enlivened by the dynamics of the reflected image of the "gaze" of the "other," the therapist as "smooth, hard surface."

In the Middle Ages the Eye of God was the divine mirror (Proverbs 7:27), albeit one which St. Augustine would say indicated man's wretchedness in the splendor of God. The medieval mirror did not duplicate reality, rather it indicated an ethereal world. Knowledge of self was a step toward God since all images exist in God. The mirror was ambivalent in that it could also be the seat of the devil in its deception and an indicator of lust, pride, vanity, and envy, as well as flaws and obligations, splendor and seduction. This ambivalence indicated a deeper sense of the mirror as inviting speculation (*specula* as the forms which make up appearance). In other words, the mirror could be seen as a medium of consideration of relationship or of dialogue between the known and the unknown, the visible and the invisible.

The Renaissance was experienced as a time when God's splendor truly inhabited the earth, a condition anticipated by Paul when he wrote, "But we all, with open face beholding as in a glass the glory of the Lord, are changed into the same image from glory to glory even as by the Spirit of the Lord."[24] Paul's first letter to Corinthians (I 13:12) had held the notion that in earthly life, we can only see "through a glass darkly," and that only "face to face" with the Lord can one truly know "even as also I am known." Focus descended from the heavens to the earth and its people as the human subject was coming into being as an object of contemplation. The individual personality was born and along with it a Hamlet like self-consciousness through the reflected image of self in the mirror. The silvered glass mirror as the eye of God was coming into wide use generally, as well as becoming an object of necessity for the aristocracy striving for an ideal appearance. The mirror, then, was a means of social organization as well as the carrier of shame of an external authority.

I am seen, therefore I am; the mirror is the gaze. But what was seen in the mirror was complex, a spectacle of multiple perspectives. St. Theresa had written, "My soul in its entirety was presented to me as in a clear mirror."[25] "Entirety" meant many aspects of the personality, many thoughts, emotions, desires, many irrationalities not under the subject's control. Indeed, one saw "someone else more than oneself," as a 15th century voice put it.[26] Sabine Melchoir-Bennet sums up the cultural event:

"By organizing and breaking up space according to an arbitrary centering, the mirror reveals the relativity of perspective and thus restores a complexity and mobility to mind play, a mirror-prism in which concepts and

images fit into one another, and graft meanings on top of
each other in a network of metaphors and references."[27]
In the Renaissance, the mirror and the sensibility of reflected
self-image allowed for a development of consciousness in which
the imagination as mediator between the visible and the unseen
presence would come to characterize self-knowledge. There is
not a "self" as much as there is a dialogue between self and other
creating the sensibility of self which finds a multiplicity of images
through the gaze of the mirror. It is this sense of the multi-layered
subject which ultimately gives rise to human personality as
multiple through the vision of depth psychology.

The Mirror in Depth Psychology

While the field of psychology has traditionally wrestled with the
dualistic notion of self as unitary phenomenon, an encapsulated
entity separate from the world, the mirror has been a guiding
metaphor in the psychology of the 20th century signifying the
interface of self/other. Freud argued that the analyst was to be
"opaque to his patients and, like a mirror, should show them
nothing but what is shown to him."[28] Jung talked about the
reflecting quality of quicksilver, or mercury, as a fundamental
quality of the psyche.[29] The radical psychoanalyst, Jacques Lacan,
formulated the idea of "a mirror stage" in an infant's development
when the infant incorporates a sense of self from its specular
image in the mirror.[30] The infant makes a "jubilant assumption"
of the specular image as a reflection of self.

Maurice Merleau-Ponty delineated the different stages of
infant development vis a vis the mirror. In the first three months
the infant shows no reaction to the mirror; at the fifth month
it reacts in a fixated way, after six months, it displays conduct
toward the specular image, at eight months it shows a reaction of
surprise. It is as if the infant has come to feel itself in an other's
body. At one year, specular images are differentiated from self as
body. At twelve to fifteen months, the image becomes part of a
game, not just a double of oneself but a sort of "witness" that the

toddler carries as part of identity. Merleau-Ponty describes the unfolding of identity in this manner as, "I am because there is a viewpoint that can be taken on me."[31]

In the tradition of psychoanalysis, the idea that identity is formed in part through the connection with a mirroring other has evolved from Freud's drive theory which postulated the existence of innate biological drives that present themselves in a priori patterns based on physical development in relation to environmental objects. I am what I am based on the relative success or failure of my psyche at crucial times in my developmental history in mediating external influences on these drives centered in oral, anal, and genital bodily zones. Subsequently, Freud's theory formulated a tripart division of the psyche into the id, ego and superego with the superego being in part the internalized influence of the outer world on instincts, which are associated with the soma or id. The ego serves as an intermediary influence, in part containing, in part separating, the two. Freud's ultimate theoretical move was to a more ego-based model, which suggests that the ego is formed under the influence of various defenses relative to anxiety stemming from internal and external sources. Freud's view always considered both constitution and environment but gradually shifted from a primary focus on instinctual drives to the ego as mediator between soma and environment as the central feature of personality.

Psychoanalytic object relations theory looks not so much to drives as the foundation of the psyche, but to the quality of the experiences of interaction the individual has with the world, especially in infancy and childhood. Sense of self comes from the experienced pleasure or displeasure one has in relation to an "other" internalized through imagination in the form of a structure or "object." Melanie Klein theorized that the infant develops self in relation to the "other" as mother's breast. This breast is either an ideal good breast, a perpetually ready source of nurturance, or a bad breast, withholding and unavailable. The infant's fantasy of good or bad breast depends upon instinctual strivings toward both connection and destruction, as well as the actual experience of the mother. The infant develops its sense of self, not only from the quality of breast but its developed ability to incorporate the impulse to devour, as well as attach to the breast. As the child develops, good and bad external objects become unified, differentiation of self and object takes place, and the coalescing of good and bad internal objects occurs. Good Mom and Bad Mom are the same; I am different from Mom; I can feel deprivation and anger and know that I will also feel gratification. A stable self-concept has emerged along with an internalized representational object world through the interlacing of instinct driven fantasy and interaction with the world.

D. W. Winnicott suggested that it is the mother's face which acts as the mirror to the infant providing its sense of self. "What does the baby see when he or she looks at the mother's face? . . . what the baby sees is himself or herself. In other words, the mother is looking at the baby and what she looks like is related to what she sees there."[32] The mothering figure acts as mediator of the infant's anxiety in the face of the world. The infant cries, the mother answers its need, and the infant sees its secure self in what Heinz Kohut would call, "the twinkle in the eye" of the mother.

For Kohut, when the infant does not experience self as the mothering person's reflection in a basically positive way, he or she becomes narcissistically wounded in the capacity to experience self positively vis a vis the environment. This condition is corrected in analysis through transference, in which the analyst becomes an ideal extension of the patient, essentially mirroring back the patient's needs, feelings and impulses. The reflection of the analyst is more like the shimmering from the surface of a body of water, revealing depths of psychological life unrecognized by the patient. The patient can then re-experience himself or herself as the "center of the universe," developing a "self-object," which can eventually distinguish between ideals and realistically achievable genuinely gratifying goals and relationships.

Following Winnicott, Thomas Ogden differentiates four aspects of the dialectical tension between infant and mother involved in the creation of the psychological subject:[33] 1) At-onement versus separation posits that true separation of infant self as subject cannot occur without a simultaneous sense of unification with the mother. There is never an "infant" rather "infant qua mother." 2) The mirroring relationship involves an "I-me" dialectic such that what either infant or mother sees in the act of mutual gaze is interdependent. The mother's mirroring allows for the infant to develop a simultaneous sense of a necessarily interacting "I" as subject and "me" as object. 3) The dialectic of creation/discovery of object involves the phenomenon of the infant's possession of "not-me" through a simultaneous creation of the object (extension of self) and discovery of what is waiting to be created. 4) The dialectic of creative/destruction involves the infant's fantasy of destroying the internal mother object as a means of discovering the external mother (subject and object). "I/me" become that, as mother is "destroyed/created."

With the formulations of Klein, Kohut, Winnicott, and Ogden we have a sense of infant and mother, each impacting the other, co-creating self and other in an interactive unit. This theoretical construct is confirmed and furthered by the actual observation of infants and mothering figures. Infant observation holds that infants are not bundles of drives in search of objects with which to cathect or matrixes of structures which have been introjected into either sufficient or deficient organizations. Rather, infants are born with capacities to actively engage with and co-create their environment with caretakers. Development proceeds through an interaction between self-regulatory and mutual regulatory processes. Self-regulation contributes to regulation and exchange but in different amounts. Within one week of birth, an infant can distinguish between the breast milk of its mother and that of another woman. Within one month an infant can discriminate the features of its mother's face and the voice quality of its mother. Within two to three months, the infant can smile responsively and gaze into the parent's eyes. Between the 7th and 9th month, the infant discovers that he or she can share another state of mind such as intention. The infant may drop its rattle and sense that by looking at the rattle in the presence of an "other," the other will also sense the loss. In other words, the infant can imaginatively impute an internal mental state to another so that it can share in joint attention to something, convey desire to have something, or react to a misreading or faulty attunement on the part of an external agent as to something the infant feels.

Disruption and repair, or non-repair, are a constantly recurring dynamic between infant and caretaker. As rupture occurs between infant and parent, the infant will strive for reparation. Depressed mothering figures are customarily described as angry, poking, intrusive, and disengaged, and their infants as protesting and disengaged. If the infant's striving for repair is not reciprocated, the infant will develop an expectation of rupture and respond accordingly, even with adequately responsive new partners. In later developmental periods, when expectations of the environment are disappointed, knowledge of reality is disavowed defensively to be replaced by an ego syntonic fantasy. In summary, infant observation suggests that infants and caretakers form a dyad from birth with the behavior of each contributing to the self-image of the other.

Who we are becomes not an internally reified entity, but an orientation to the world which covers a wide range of possibilities. Using Merleau-Ponty's word, identity is a "conduct" in relation to a context, a way of "grasping" the world as it presents itself, a "mode" of reciprocity to the world. Psychoanalysis furthers this sense of identity formation with its foundation in imagination, a psychic agency with little representation in infant observation. The other as mirror does not reflect a literal picture, rather perception is always "dark," that is manifest through an aesthetic process or fantasy, an interpretation. What is "there," and therefore "here," is always a co-creation between external and internal, between imagination and an objective source. The "I" that I "am" is always an image or a narrative created through the inter-relationship of inner and outer.

In this chapter, we have expanded the metaphor of wounded healer from the previous chapter to explore the inter-relational nature of the psyche in terms of the inherent connection of self/

other in creating a subject revolving around the metaphor of mirror reflection. We have seen that what is traditionally represented as a substantial core of being, a self, is more psychologically imaged in terms of mutual reflection. These explorations point to an extended gaze on the subjective self, not just as a mirror reflection of an other, or the liminal space of a reciprocal reflection of self/other, but a darkened image of the mirror cracked by the lens of imagination. What emerges from imagination is not just a single image, but a kaleidoscopic "wilderness" of multiple simultaneous images in continuous revolution that has no final resting place.

Out of the Mirror emerges the Many . . .

Endnotes

[1] Jung, C. G., "The Psychology of the Transference," in *The Practice of Psychotherapy*, CW16, p. 234.

[2] Merleau-Ponty, M., "The Child's Relation to Others" in *The Primacy of Perception*, p. 136.

[3] *Ibid*, 185.

[4] The head is traditionally the "seat of the soul" so that the severed head indicates an autonomous being. In Mayan culture, the mythical original ballgame is played with a severed head as the ball alluding to the autonomous life of the ball itself.

[5] Esslin, M., *The Theatre of the Absurd*, p. 142.

[6] *Ibid*, p. 140.

[7] Sartre, J. P., *Being and Nothingness: an Essay on Phenomenological Ontology*, p. 272.

[8] Van Gough wanted his portraits to be seen as if they were aberrations.

[9] Lacan, J., "Seminar on the 'Purloined Letter'" in *Escrit: A Selection*. See also John P. Muller and W. J. Richardson Eds, *The Purloined Poe*.

[10] Sartre, p. 285.

[11] Jung, C. G., "The Practical Use of Dream Analysis" in *The Practice of Psychotherapy*, CW16, p. 145.

[12] Buber, M., *I and Thou*, p. 59.

[13] *Ibid*, p. 55.

[14] *Ibid*, p. 55.

[15] *Ibid*, p. 59.

[16] *Ibid*, p. 63.

[17] *Ibid*, p. 62.

[18] *Ibid*, p. 76.

[19] *Ibid*, p. 80.

[20] *Ibid*, p. 83.

[21] *Ibid*, p. 84.

[22] Melchior-Bonnet, S., The Mirror: A History.

[23] Plato, "Pheaedrus" (255 c-d) in *The Collected Dialogues of Plato*, p. 501.

[24] II Corinthians 3:18.

[25] Melchior-Bonnet, p. 126.

[26] *Ibid*, p. 17.

[27] *Ibid*, p. 129.

[28] Freud, S., "Recommendations to Physicians Practicing Psycho-analysis" in *Standard Edition*, 12, p. 118.

[29] Jung, C. G., "The Spirit Mercurius" in *Alchemical Studies*, CW 13.

[30] Lacan, J., "The mirror stage as formative of the function of the I as revealed in psychoanalytic experience," in *Escrits*.

[31] Merleau-Ponty, M., "The Child's Relations to Others." in *The Primacy of Perception*, p. 136.

[32] Winnicott, D. W., "Mirror Role of Mother and Family in Child Development" in *Playing and Reality*, p. 112.

[33] Ogden, T., *Subjects of Analysis*.

Chapter Eight

The Fiery Furnace/The Sacred Bath

The Art of the Fugue in Psychotherapy

Imagine that as an analyst, you have retrieved your patient, and settling into your chair as the patient settles into his or her couch or chair, you lean back to listen....the patient starts in and you hear the first note of Bach's Concerto for Four Keyboards (adapted from Vivaldi). In the beginning, you hear a single note on the downbeat, held for a beat and a half, followed by the same note on a subsequent downbeat, followed by a downbeat note, this time a harmonious interval above the original note, followed by two notes of the original pitch only now, one is off beat, and one is on, and this latter sequence is repeated. The original note is then repeated several times on the downbeat with a rapid succession of notes in between leading into the downbeat. There follows a conclusive series of three notes taking us to a pitch five steps below and in harmony with the original pitch. The musical line has journeyed up and down the pitch scale at different rhythms to finally get to the emphatic, central keynote. All the notes before this central note were preparation leading us to it, and they all sound related to each other as if they are harmonious parts of the same group.

Now imagine the central keynote is a tone that carries an emotion, and the notes above it are expansions of that tone followed by a line of consciousness that is eventually pulled by its strength down to its foundation. Then this line of music/emotional tones is complemented by another voice as a "countersubject" emotion, either above or below the original in tone. Another line as voice appears, then another, and so on until you have eight lines of music, several emotional voices all resounding in conjunction with the others. In addition, an orchestra emphasizes certain points in the piece with amplifications of its own as well as answering the melodic line with its responses. Imagine the orchestral accompaniment as emanating from the psyche of oneself as therapist. As a line tumbles down the scale, it is "caught" and held by an orchestral chord, or as a line strives ever upward the orchestra will hold it at a climactic point, or the orchestra will respond to a series of notes with its own adaptation—all internalized within the therapist's psyche.

Back to the melodic line of the patient: as one line expresses an emotional tone, another will counter or amplify with gradations of that tone. As one line takes an upward course, another will descend and vice versa, giving a grounding in contrast to aerial flights. As one slows down, another will speed up, as one becomes softer, the other louder, one silent, another enters, and so on. Each line alternatively might become more emotional or more reflective or thoughtful in relation to another. Sometimes, when the subject voice reaches a note five steps above its original central note, another voice will come in five steps below with each progressing upward or downward to resolve in a single note. Sometimes, the subject line will require a series of ascents or descents to reach its ultimate pinnacle or nadir. Sometimes, the relationships of different notes in a chord will be explored by one or more than one line, and sometimes one or more lines will go off into different keys. Sometimes, the explorations will be tentative and others, confident. The constant is that while each line is always independent of the others, it is always in relation to the others creating a complex form of conversation among several voices.

The different voices of music may be imagined as "streams of consciousness," or psychic reverberations, appearing in the patient and in analyst, some loud and dominating, others soft, barely audible, as the patient explores different aspects and levels of the current psychological terrain. Listening to the patient, many voices are heard at once. "Doctor" hears the content of "patient's" main theme: a large issue—problem with relationship, work, or family, amplified by small, metaphorically related variations - annoyances with traffic, fantasies regarding an attractive passer-by, or thoughts as to the evening meal.

The content of the initial presentation, the first "note," is not the actual core of the issue rather it is a signifier. The analyst needs to be led by the patient's consciousness along a stream to get to the core. Meanwhile, other voices make their entrance from the analyst's unconscious scanning to find connection to the patient's flow—complementary situations in the analyst's relationship, work, and family; echoes of the last session along with noteworthy changes in emotional tone; reverberations from the patient's past history in similar situations and noted patterns; reflections from analyst's own history of similar situations; glimpses of universal patterns and images in the patient's daily experience; theoretical constructs; emotional stirrings; and bodily adumbrations—all presenting themselves through the analyst's own psychic instrumentation.

The second movement of the concerto adds further complexity. At a slower tempo, it starts with solid melodic chords in preparation for something new and different, a discovery, a surprise. A base line provides a sustained note to maintain the fundamental tonality. Then, at the right moment (*kairos*,), a single right hand moves over into the upper reaches of the register on the keyboard for a prolonged period of tender, tremulous exploration. The sound is poignant, poetic, a birth of sorts, a new possibility unfolding, a mystery. A transformation is taking place.

Likewise, in our patient, the tone may turn to another key in a new field for which we can only have intuitions because it is located at a deep, and barely perceptible level. Something is coming together in the patient while at the same time signaling a new focus in the analytic relationship, a third psyche enveloping the two originals, underneath and above, the unconscious interactions between and conjunctions of a two-person un-conscious—father to daughter, mother to son, etc. Then, a new voice seems to enter the field independent of the detectable voices of patient and doctor, but informing them of a more profound world between the two while encompassing both. At an even deeper level, archetypal voices are making themselves heard, voices common to the ancestry of the human condition. The musical field has now become extremely complex with foreground and background, personal and archetypal, subjective and objective all intermingling into an encompassing, "larger-than" space or a full-bodied concerto.

Beginning Condition

As a young man my problems needed a container in which to be held. I started with what was at hand—my own analysis, my own need for security, and my interest in and curiosity about others with problems. I decided to make psychotherapy my work with an orientation toward understanding the meaning carried by psychopathology. I came to see work with patients as providing a reflection of my problems, an objective corollary to my internal, autonomous, ongoing self-healing process.[1] Together we worked to extract a meaning, shared by the two of us which forces of nature and reason had held in abeyance through defense and resistance, a work against nature.

I meet my patient for the hour and we proceed to the office. I am interested in the look on the face, the tone of physical movement and the general demeanor. Like attracts like, so what about this individual attracts or repels me at this particular time, and what about me attracts or repels this person? We mutually need each other, contain each other. Each quality evokes, or creates to an extent, a complementary quality in the other, setting up a dyadic structure. I am the doctor to the patient, the patient, the wounded to my healer. I represent empowerment and strength to the patient's felt sense of disempowerment and weakness, the patient, ignorance to my knowledge. I create the office space, the patient comes to my door; the patient pays the fee, I collect it. I listen. This is the beginning structure, power by necessity tilted my way, and if the session is successful, it will meander its way around to a different configuration.

Sacrifice

For movement to occur, a sacrifice must be made. The patient has already paid the sacrifice by coming to my door and agreeing on a fee. Now it is my turn. As doctor, I give up. For the moment I am blank—no title, no knowledge, no memory, no desire, nothing to impart or educate with, *neti*, *neti*, not this, not that—only curiosity. The adventure is to encounter this person as completely as possible, starting with what is at hand. Freud's classic opening question is, what is on your mind? The patient sounds the first note, and I am especially interested in the first words—"Blah, blah, blah blah blah."…. or "no words" (as some patients have begun). Pause, silence…and then my first internal reactions. There follows the narrative, harmonious or chaotic, spoken or unspoken, with its peaks and vales, its fast and slow, its cries and whispers, and I am drawn in, caught, had, done, by the patient.

Descent: The Bloody Hand

As the patient begins, things start to happen. Thought leads to thought, image to image, feeling to feeling, fantasy to fantasy. Characters are brought in—relational partners, family members, work relationships, friends, and acquaintances. Memories are evoked, history unfolded, amplifications made, this is like that. A process is starting, which can be thought of as a journey, a movement over ground or as cooking event, stationary, covered over the heat. As a journey, a descent is occurring; as cooking, a baking or stirring-up or blending or dissolving. Either way, the patient is losing it, dropping into something else, at once more painful and more comforting, more strengthening, and more weakening, more enlightening and more darkening.

. . . Or not. Every step downwards is resisted in one way or another. It is how the patient has survived. Now, the opening provided by the presence of the analyst is pulling it up and that is painful. Each resistance provides the analyst for an opening: when the rhythm is altered, or a word is out of place or repeated or especially poetic or poignant, or a behavior out of sync with the throughline of the narrative, or a feeling emerges that seems incongruent. Why this? Why that? And then, the spherical process starts all over on a new level, each time around, a little different.

Something similar is happening with the doctor. As the patient drops into his or her wounds, the doctor's internal radar scans his/ her personal unconscious for connections with patient's unconscious, and he/she sinks into the related wounds or associations. Evoked are similar thoughts, feelings, and fantasies, corresponding relational situations with marriages, friends, family and work colleagues, songs and stories, images of personal mayhem and associations from movies, etc. The doctor is *with* the patient in the field, and each association, each new thought, feeling or fantasy, is now a mutual creation revealing a new image. Part of this psychological action is overt, most is covert, flowing by, under the radar, passed back and forth under the table.

A counter movement starts to occur in patient and doctor, a resistance in the relationship. The doctor doesn't want to give up being the healer, the patient doesn't want to give up the comfort of the invalid. These counter movements are carried within each in response to both personal and inter-subjectival process. As the patient or doctor sinks, there may be a counter movement upward within the patient or the doctor, each depression countered by a tendency toward mania, each despair reacted to with desire, each doubt, coupled with a certainty. Both doctor and patient, feeling unease at a certain level, may find a way to discharge, or bleed off, the anxiety—to direct the discourse away from the source of his or her discomfort.

At the same time, what had always been latent, comes more to the surface in that each party becomes part of the other's story, the bloody finger painting on the ball's face in between becomes mutual creation. While the patient had consciously focused his or her narrative on characters in a personal life which indirectly had a connection with the analyst, now the analyst is created into an active, overt part of the story. What was father, mother, husband, wife, partner, boss, subordinate, now is created from the personage of the analyst. At the same time, the patient starts to have a special meaning for the therapist, taking the place of significant others in the therapist's life. The patient's anger becomes that of the therapist's father, a pull for affection, his mother. Each of the two individuals become objects for the other's envy, jealousy, love, hate, affection or disgust. A subliminal bipolar field has been formed, which can be used as a barometer of the emotional climate in the room. Chaos or deadness, conjunction or correlation from the couple below the surface may envelop the two above, anger or eros, need or guilt, hunger or overfill, inflation or fear, merger or distance.

The Analytic Supper

While this sort of inter-relational dynamic is going on all the time in the analytic setting, the extreme of a inter-subjective relationship occurs when one of the parties, usually the patient, feels an intensity of affect that is intolerable.[2] At that point, the patient will find a means, as if to inject or deposit the feeling into the therapist. The therapist will be feeling something for which he or she cannot find a source and become confused. The patient may then manipulate the situation, so that the therapist acts out the feeling. The patient has then successfully found a container for the intolerable feeling, at once allowing the feeling to find a life in the space and being relieved of having to suffer it.

What may happen now is an enactment by the therapist, in the moment or later. To avoid the painful feeling, a mode of diversion will be found—changing the subject on the patient, cutting him or her off, ending the session prematurely, forgetting the patient's name, offering a literal hand for connection, introducing a new or different technique such as asking for dreams, forgetting or changing the time of the next session, stalling on providing information for insurance reimbursement, raising the fee without prior notice, agreeing to cutting back on sessions or even terminating altogether. In another sense, the therapist will try to make the relationship an arena in which he or she has the power to gratify the patient's various desires—engaging in socially acceptable surface conversation, accepting gifts without inquiring as to their meaning, engaging in didactic or educational activity, giving advice, contacting or meeting the patient outside the therapeutic hour—in short, leaving the therapist's chair. The patient, at some level, will have the accurate sense that the therapist cannot tolerate what the patient is bringing forward and will collude with the therapist in unconscious avoidance and flight toward comfort.

A scene in the film, "Silence of the Lambs," depicts the stark underlying dynamics of the analytic couple. The protagonist, Hannibal Lecter, is a psychopathic psychiatrist, who literally eats his patients. He is imprisoned and being treated by a sadistic prison psychologist. The scene depicts the prison psychologist on the couch, as if now the "patient," indulging himself with hostile fantasy regarding Lecter, while his patient, the imprisoned doctor, is strapped and gagged, while seated behind the head of the psychologist as if his psychoanalyst, unspeaking and unmoving, while the sadistic psychologist/patient tears him down verbally.

The scene illustrates certain truths about psychoanalysis. In a way, the analyst does "eat" the patient, in that the doctor must "take in" what the patient serves, digest it, and present it in a form in which it can be reintegrated. The doctor will insert clarifying interventions, and at the same time, suffer masochistically the aggression of the patient. Likewise, the therapeutic field is at times fraught with erotic energy from both the patient and the therapist in relation to the instincts and unmet needs of each engendered by the intimacy of the field. Therapist and patient awaken appetites for suffering, eros, and power in each other through underlying personal ingredients in dishes served to each other at the analytic dinner table.

The Fiery Furnace/The Sacred Bath

The characterization of the analytic relationship as a dinner for two is a metaphor for what is always going on between the therapist and patient in an underlying connection. It is describing a "third world" consisting of the interaction of the personal unconscious dynamics between the two parties. The analyst's unconscious perpetrator will inevitably draw out and interact with the patient's unconscious victim and vice versa, the patient's hidden starvation and depletion with the therapist's over abundant force feeder, the therapist's concealed thief with what is envied in the patient, the patient's overzealous parent to the therapist's deprived child, the therapist's fire to the patient's malaise, the patient's self-aggrandizer to the therapist's self-deprecator, the therapist's aggression to the patient's guilt, the patient's seducer to the therapist's need for love, the therapist's greed to the patient's sense of deprivation. Finally, these hidden qualities may latch on to mutual eros to make themselves manifest in disguised form. This third agency in the therapeutic field is like an imaginal body, a third entity, a third agent or a third person, as if that voice, which originally called the two parties together in seemingly perverse, mutually unconscious, therapeutic alliance.

The goal of the therapist is to "see" the sequestered feeling and enable its expression—to mirror it, in such a way that is not threatening to the patient. The patient can then experience the feeling, and together with the therapist, explore its meaning. Gradually, the patient is then able to digest what was once regurgitated. Herein lies the fundamental ethic of psychotherapy: in the analytic moment, to honor the encounter as an endeavor toward meaning which can ultimately enable the realization of potential in the individual personality. The doctor must be able to discern in some manner what belongs to the doctor, and what to the patient, and make the former palatable. The therapist needs to let herself be used, to be able to take on and hold the image into which the patient creates her to eventually mutually discover its meaning.

The means, or mode, or medium through which this "subtle body" is best accessed, the medium of the therapeutic endeavor par excellence, is a subjunctive, "as if" mode of fantasy, reverie and imagination. It is an intermediary space between subject and object. It is a way of seeing and experiencing such that relationship becomes a "world," imaginatively co-created and partaking of both tangible and intangible It is what in Sufi mythology is called the "imaginal world" between spirit and matter, and partaking of each, but encompassing both. The Sufis thought of it as the ultimate goal, a "place of no-place," unable to be fixed by literal interpretations or spiritual maps and achieved only at the point of letting go all will and expectation regarding achievement. Imagination occurs at the cost of the comfort of rationality and willfulness. Using fantasy and imagination, it is as if the therapist can feelingly "see" emotions flowing between therapist and patient and ultimately give voice to them. As inhabitants of a "third world," doctor and patient can walk the snake-like path, at times torturous, at times sublime, toward an unknown "destination," which paradoxically ultimately takes on the aspect of the analytic process itself.

Harkening back to Buber's sense of "I/Thou," C. G. Jung picks up on the sensibility of the "intimations of eternity" as it holds in the psychotherapeutic relationship. "(T)he soul cannot exist without its other side, which is always found in a 'You.' Wholeness is a combination of I and You, and these show themselves to be parts of a transcendent unity."[3] This unity inevitably makes its appearance in the therapeutic relationship. "The analytical work must inevitably lead sooner or later to a fundamental discussion between 'I' and 'You' and 'You' and 'I' on a plane stripped of all human pretenses"[4] as if analyst and patient find themselves together in what can feel like a furnace of tumult or a bath of resolution. Jung describes this interface as an alchemical process of mutual transformation:

"For two personalities to meet is like mixing two different chemical substances: if there is any combination at all, both are transformed. In any effective psychological treatment, the doctor is bound to influence the patient;

but this influence can only take place if the patient has a reciprocal influence on the doctor . . . The patient influences him unconsciously . . . and brings about changes in the doctor's unconscious . . .."[5]

Jung is sensitive to the confusion, darkness, and chaos that is an important part of the experience in the encounter of the healing relationship. The therapist develops a "personal" connection to the patient, becomes "fascinated" and therapist and patient find themselves in mutual unconsciousness.[6] Both are led to a direct confrontation with the daemonic forces lurking in the darkness. The resultant paradoxical blend of positive and negative, of trust and fear, of hope and doubt, of attraction and repulsion, is characteristic of the original, *ur*, relationship. It is the hate and love of the elements which the alchemists likened to the primeval chaos.[7] The situation is enveloped in a kind of "fog," what alchemists call "blacker than black," and the experience is one of "impenetrable chaos."[8] Jung declared that in this aspect of therapy, the doctor is like the alchemist who doesn't know if he is the alchemist working over the fire, or the salamander burning in the vessel.[9] Jung's emphasis is that for the individual psyche to become whole, it seeks an "other" to carry those aspects of itself which it can't consciously hold.

To summarize the different simultaneously present realms of the analytic dyad as delineated in the present and previous chapters:

A) The analytic couple relate to each other through their respective personas as doctor and patient.

B) Patient becomes aware of personal wounds, doctor aware of professional capabilities.

C) Doctor and patient relocate their stories into the other.

D) Doctor becomes aware of personal wounds; patient becomes aware of personal strengths.

E) The personal unconscious dynamics of doctor and patient interact.

F) The entire configuration is grounded in the agency of the archetypal wounded healer.

Re-membering the Little Mermaid[10]

Undine (Ltn. *Undda* for "wave") is the name Paracelsus, the alchemist philosopher of the German Renaissance, gave to spirits associated with the element water, in turn part of a larger category of invisible counterparts of the four elements in Nature, each living in their distinct worlds. The undine is the personification, energy or life of water in all of its forms. This idea is descended from Greek mythology in which Nereids are the attendants of Poseidon and Oceanides govern the waters of the world. The Greeks thought of water as a female element and undines are usually female, the most well-known being mermaids.

As narratives evolved around the undine as mermaid, she became associated with a soulless condition and thereby, condemned to yearning to be free of the void in her water-logged existence—tears as the appearance of the bitter salt water of the sea. A soul could only emerge for the undine through love and unification with a mortal in earthly life. The ensouled mermaid would then be living a human life, albeit with an essence of a different order. The conditions of her existence were that if she was betrayed by her lover, she would have to kill him and return to the water. The undine comes to meet her mortal lover by rescuing him from water in some form and saving him from suffocation by giving him breath. She makes her appearance arising out of water to love or to kill.

As an alternative to the Disneyfication of the story, another version emerges and carries us into deeper, darker waters: the German film, "Undine" (2020), directed by Christian Petzold. The film is about human relationship and its vicissitudes— seeing the other and being seen, connection and rupture, trust and betrayal, emerging and disappearing, ultimately different forms of living and dying, while beautifully weaving imagery from the legend into everyday life. If we see through the mythic narrative and its imagery, we might imagine a depiction of the analytic relationship, in that the film reveals the concealed dual nature of the dynamic between undine and mortal. Mortal desires as undine desires, and their mutual desiring allows for the appearance of each, as well as their mutual distrust bringing about the rupture and disappearance of each.

The film's illustration of interrelationship reflects the underlying unconscious interaction between conscious and unconscious, as well as patient and analyst.[11] We know that the undine needs to be seen and loved by a mortal in order to have a soul and human life "out of water." We can see in this scenario the desire of an element of unconsciousness to appear to consciousness, and at the same time, the modern analytic patient in search of a soul from below. The realization of an essential self, emergent out of the depths of unconsciousness, is yearning to be seen and accepted (loved) by an other (the analyst). The counter yearning of the analyst can be seen in terms of unconscious desires that are addressed through work with patients. What we look for in the film's version of the fairy tale is the inter-related action, "under the surface," that exists between conscious and unconscious, and between patient and analyst, as modeled by the undine and her mortal lover.

The film opens on the face of a "mermaid" named Undine, a contemporary young woman sitting at an outdoor coffee table in Berlin, struggling with her married lover, Johannes, to make an eye-to-eye connection. There is controversy as to who initiated the meeting: Undine with the words, "We have to meet," or Johannes "I have to see you," indicative of the ambivalent interweaving of their underworlds. A break-up is occurring in this affair, and he is returning to his wife. She tells him that if he leaves, she will kill him, ominous words from an undine. It is she who then leaves to attend to her duties as a public lecturer, admonishing Johannes to be at the table when she returns.

The relationship has ruptured. Undine's misguided effort to be "seen" and loved has led to a flawed object, a dead end analogous to the situation in analysis when an unconscious collusion or coasting between analyst and patient produces a stasis or rupture in the process. There is mutual avoidance of something misfiring or too intense to acknowledge, which the patient is unconsciously struggling to get the analyst to see, but consciousness cannot tolerate the unconscious content.

As Undine walks to her destination across the street, she is accompanied by the beginning sublime strains of the Adagio to Bach's keyboard concerto in D Minor (bvd 974). The melody flows with a rising line echoing the passion of the undine, and ultimately alternates with a counterpoint descent reflecting the undine's disappointed yearning. The beat of the baseline emphasizes persistence in her quest. In fact, the composers of the Baroque era held D minor to emphasize a mixture of the two emotional tones of the undine—gravity with a soft gaiety, devotion along with a natural flowing, tenderness with "melancholy womanliness."

Undine's job—telling for a mythical inhabitant of watery depths—is historian of urban development and the emergence of the city of Berlin ("The Marsh"). She is a therapist to the soul of the city. Just before her talk, she looks down through a window from above—a distanced bird's eye view—at Johannes standing while talking on the phone, presumably to his wife. Her "gaze" of desire has now taken two forms—up close and painfully personal, and through a glass from above paralleling the forth and back flow of analytic relationship. The film will depict the ins and outs, ups and downs, of attempted connection through scenes of arrival and departures, but also through eye-to-eye contact versus through a lens of glass (darkly).

Undine gives her lecture while looking down on a miniature model of Berlin's inner city—a talk which brings in another variation on the theme of finding soul—the core or center of a living being, city or human, remains consistent over time amid the changes that go on at the periphery. Undine's presentations focus upon the variances in attitude toward the Palace Center of Berlin across the centuries. Originally built in the 15th century, it took several forms, which were finalized during the beginning of the 18th century German Baroque (the same time period Bach was composing, and the undine legend emerged). The Palace at first was on the outskirts of the urban area but gradually took on a central location as the metropolis moved out and around it. World War II brought destruction, and under the East German government the area became a "wasteland." Ultimately, after Reunification in 1989-90, and several years of debate, the original ancient form of the Palace was restored utilizing modern technology. We can imagine this discourse to be the parallel between the historical life of the Palace as evolving "center" (soul) in relation to the city, and the emergence of the human soul sought after by the undine through relationship. It gradually becomes a center of a developing context, then is destroyed and finally re-emerges, its core qualities remain intact as it appears and disappears under different conditions. While pointing to the model, Undine asks her audience the crucial question of historians, lovers, and analytical pairs, "Where are we?" and the camera pans to the empty coffee table down the street awaiting Undine.

Then, things become interesting. In psychoanalysis, when there is stalemate in the process, underlying pressure on the container accrues, and there is ultimately an explosion (expression of rage, early ending of a session or even termination) or emotional implosion (enactment by either analyst or patient). Ideally, containment is restored through mutual rescue and the analyst's repair through sharing an understanding of the mutual unconsciousness and the underlying psychological intentions revealed in the incident. Undine, in search of her lover, returns to the café, does not find him, goes inside, extends her search to the men's room, and symbolically turns off the water faucet left running there. Back in the dining area inside, Undine hears her name (call to the mermaid,) looks up and sees a water-filled aquarium perched on the top of a cabinet with the model of a diver underwater as if *it* had made the call. She hears her name again, this time coming from a young man, Christoph, who is in search of her. He himself *is* an industrial diver, who works in the underwater infrastructure of the city, has attended her lectures, and would like to learn more from her. During their conversation, the diver (out of water) clumsily backs into the cabinet and the aquarium teeters and falls. Undine (the mermaid) rushes forward and pushes Christoph away, rescuing him from serious harm while getting cut herself. In turn, he takes care of her, pulling out the glass shards, the two watery beings, now on dry land, lying on the floor, face-to-face in attachment, and the broken nearby diver model as fetish is retrieved.

The traditional narrative has been turned around. There has been another break-up, this time a break-through—the container holding the model diver (mortal) under water (unconscious) is smashed, freeing the diver (model/mortal) now literally at hand and accessible. The undine (patient) has rescued the mortal, but the mortal (analyst) turns out to be at home underwater diver). Mortal/diver/analyst tends to undine/patient/unconsciousness in return for her rescue of him. The dynamic between patient and analyst is now revealed to go two ways in terms of searching, finding, rescuing, and being found/ seen/loved.

The scene shifts to the diver at work underwater, tending to infrastructure. He marks the name "Undine" on an iron brace but then comes eye-to-eye with a legendary giant catfish, Gunther, that no one has seen before. Here, the diver/analyst is working on the psychological infrastructure under water (unconscious,) coming to a core "Undine" element, along with her totem animal (self object) from the psychological depths. The next scene is a coming together, the arrival of Undine by train being met by Christoph. The two are now revealed as lovers separated by the glass of the train window, that which brings them together also keeps them apart, as does the analytic container for patient and analyst. The two lovers are next in bed, and the diver has descended to a different depth, under the sheets to administer cunnilingus ("going down"), and, ironically, tells her, "Now you can go back into the water," prophetic words for a mermaid on land.

We see them diving together; they look at each other face to face now through the clear plastic of their diving masks. He shows her the marked word "Undine" and a heart, but Undine disappears; her oxygen mask has detached. Gunther appears, and she is seen holding on to him, as if he is taking her away, back to her underwater home. Christian retrieves her and performs CPR (to the rhythm of the BGs "Stayin' Alive"), the mermaid now rescued by the mortal and revived with *his* breath. There is an aspect in this sequence of "joining with" in the analytic relationship, mutual exploration of the underlying dynamics and discovery of essence (name "Undine,") but the pull of unconscious dynamics is too great, and patient is pulled back into psychic depths without capability of maintaining, creating the analyst into the retriever.

The rhythm of rupture and repair continues. Undine is awaiting departure at the railroad station, but Christoph falls asleep on her shoulder (mortal/analyst unconsciousness). As the train pulls out, it is as when it arrived, connection through windows. This time, Christoph has presented Undine with the transitional object of the relationship, the model of the diver, as fetish. Cut to Undine's lecture on historical Berlin, its violent ruptures and re-gatherings with the Palace as its core, attempting establishment on swampland, paralleling the relationship of two individuals, which in turn reflects that of unconscious to consciousness, analyst and patient. The communist regime of the Cold War attempts to build a nationalist form for the people, which only results in the palace area turning to depletion— what happens when the analytic relationship reverts to a solely theoretical basis. Form must follow function for it to work, the lecturer notes but also asks, if that is the case, can there ever be progress? How often does that question come up in relationship— personal and analytical, with the ultimate response—you work with what is there. Now, it is Christoph who must leave as the two separate one more time on the station platform, the connection ruptured again. As in analysis, it is as if the arrivals and departures, connections and disconnects, are what keep the relationship going.

Johannes reappears (the arrival of a repressed complex). Again, dissatisfied with his marriage, he wants another try with Undine, and waits at the very table he had previously left An earlier chance encounter apparently has aroused Undine's guilt, despite her belief that she "can't live" without Christoph's love (mermaid's fate) symbolized by her accidentally breaking the diver model Christoph has given her. We then come upon Undine in her apartment listening to "Stayin' Alive," when she gets a "call," apparently from Christoph expressing his suspicions about her and hanging up (double disconnect).

Undine goes to the site where Christoph is working and finds that he had suffered an accident and is brain dead. Now, the story goes totally "under the below" in a very psychologically authentic way that is true to the myth. The accident, it turns out, had occurred hours *before* Undine had received his "call." In other words, she heard his voice while he was actually in a coma. Undine now, is left as jilted mermaid suffering the guilt of *her* own unfaithful feelings. She must fulfill her promise to Johannes; she goes to his house and kills him—as a mermaid must: by arising out of water (his pool) and taking his breath away. She then returns to water herself and just as she submerges, Christoph miraculously awakens from his coma. Here, we have an example of the kind of under the surface, synchronistic connection that exists and manifests not only in personal relationships and between patient and analyst, but in every moment when internal and external are in fact connected. When the unconscious of the patient, altered by consciousness but still claiming its own ground, redeems a betrayal (return of the denied complex), it can re-turn to its home in the depths. This allows the analyst to awaken from his or her own complex. Christoph attempts to find Undine but only discovers stains of wine (as if blood) spilled from a glass he had broken in her old apartment, as the signifier or trace that remains of her and their relationship. In turn, the stain of a trace can be imagined as what is left of each analytical hour.

Two years later, while working underwater at the site of his initial underwater encounter with Undine and her subsequent disappearance into the water, we see the hand of Undine appear and touch Christoph's gloved hand. Later that night, he goes back into the water and calls for Undine (call to the mermaid). As he enters its depths without diving gear, she appears, and they can authentically connect, not through lens of glass, but directly hand in hand. Christoph reappears on shore, this time with the fetish he had given Undine and she had taken with her: the model diver. The analytic truth reflected here is that only when the analyst leaves behind the accoutrements of rational, dryland, day-to-day subjectivity and theoretical orientation, and enters the underworld, the depths of unconscious life which is home to his patient, can an authentic psychological engagement be possible.

The film, "Undine," depicts a story on many levels interacting simultaneously indicating a fundamental mode of the psyche. Mythically, it is the legend of the undine, or mermaid, in search of her soul. Culturally, it is the story of the emergence of a city withstanding centuries of change with its core intact. Psychologically, it is the story of personal relationship and its vicissitudes. Now we are adding to this matrix the process of psychoanalysis and it's structuring according to the undine legend as a process of individuation through a healing relationship and intrapsychic realignment of consciousness and unconscious. What emerges is an image of subjectivity operating within a complexity of several interacting, autonomous systems— of vanishing and appearing, of phantoms and flesh, of traces and mechanics, of detachment and connection, of drowning and rescue—in short, an image of psychological life as one of multiple agencies—each with a life of its own, structured within unpredictable, asymmetrical forms. Like the little girl in a haiku, or the mermaid, or the diver—try as we might, we'll never catch the butterfly—an effort to be explored in the next chapter.

Out of the Fire emerges the Pan . . .

151

Endnotes

[1] Jung wrote that the biggest problem of the patient is the personality of the analyst and Harold Searles thought that what keeps bringing the patient back is the need to cure the analyst.

[2] Ogden, "Projective Identification and the Subjugating Third."

[3] Jung, C. G., "The Psychology of the Transference" in *The Practice of Psychotherapy*, CW 16, pp. 244-5.

[4] Jung, "Introduction to the Religious and Psychological Problems of Alchemy" in *Psychology and Alchemy*, CW 12, p. 5.

[5] Jung, "Problems in Modern Psychotherapy," in *The Practice of Psychotherapy*, CW 16, p. 71.

[6] Jung, "The Psychology of the Transference," p. 176.

[7] *Ibid*, p. 182

[8] *Ibid*, p. 187.

[9] *Ibid*, p. 199.

[10] A version of this section appeared in the journal *Psychological Perspectives*, 2023.

[11] The film, in turn reflects Jung's use of imagery in the pre-Paracelsian "Rosarium," the alchemical wedding, which arises out of the mercurial fountain. See Jung, C. G. (1954b).

Chapter 9

Slipping into the Swamp[1]

"Dee" was a woman in her early 60's, married and divorced three times with grown children, living alone, and for some time unemployed. She worked for several years as an administrator of service organizations and educational institutions. Having gained control over an addiction to food, she was still active as a sponsor with Overeaters Anonymous. A long-term relationship ended eight years prior to this analysis, and she had been without relationship since then. She entered analysis wanting to work on issues with her father, eight months deceased after an extended period of care by the patient. Her relationships with men had been marked by extreme dependency and compliance on her part, and her work life had come to a standstill due to a minimum of self-confidence, and an overriding sense of incapability. Dee presented as anxious, and in a state of overall "stuckness" in her life with periodic bouts of severe depression marked by a withdrawn state of existence in an "abyss" with minimal motivation or sense of self.

Family History

Dee was the middle child in a family of three daughters raised by her father, who ran a construction business, and her mother, a housewife. Her mother had been molested by her own father, was highly temperamental, emotionally dependent on her husband, and at times hysterical to the point of being in complete denial of reality. She was unable to connect with Dee except as an object representing her own inferiority, shame, and "wrongness." Mother related to patient through criticism, denigration, and punishment—in effect, a mother who was not only devouring, but whose presence represented the absence of a nurturing, mirroring, holding caretaker. At the same time, her mother gave Dee the underlying message that she, Dee, alone of the family members, was to take care of mother—in essence, be the mother to her mother. Dee was thus put in an intolerably double binding spiral in relation to mother—you're wrong—take care of me, you're wrong to think I need care, take care of me, etc. The result for Dee was a sense of being drained of all energy and a feeling of emptiness, that ultimately was "medicated" with a compulsion for overeating, which "gripped (her) by the neck." The seemingly unbreakable tie to her mother, through this self-negating dynamic might be seen in Dee's dependence on a small, but regular stipend from a family trust controlled by mother, which on the one hand, gratified her underlying need to be "fed" ("owed to") by her mother, but at the same time, kept her "in chains."

Dee's father was a rigid, militaristic authoritarian, who monopolized "reality" with only his perspective carrying any validity in the family. For him, the patient was failed in living up to his cliché'd, homogenous vision of what a woman should be: someone like her mother, totally dependent and compliant, without will or intelligence. Dee's native intelligence was deemed irrelevant or "crazy" by her father, rendering her without psychological "hands" with which to create a place in the family or in the world. (She suffered from a chronic condition of infirmity in her lower arms and hands.) Dee took to relating to men from a self-negating position of making herself small, such that, the man carried total power of knowledge and authority.

Dee's older sister became the favorite of the father; her younger sister aligned with the mother. Dee was left out as a recognized individual with a place in the family and resorted to defensive measures such as dressing like a boy in rebellious defiance of her parents' sense of femininity. Rage became her expression of the injustice perpetrated onto her through the family dynamics wherein she could do nothing right. Archetypally, she could be seen as a family scapegoat but also as the Orphan, the unwanted agent, the core of whom is unseen and who goes unclaimed.

Despite the deleterious effects of her family, Dee was able to raise two boys in the context of a troubled marriage, as well as work as director of non-profit projects for the disadvantaged, which were highly successful. She could experience joy and delight, be emotionally warm and sensitive, display a well-developed sense of humor, and employ a differentiated intelligence and psychological mind based on intuition.

Assessment and Goal of Treatment

At the beginning of our analytic encounter, Dee's psychological structure included severe depression and a periodic extreme withdrawn defensive mode. She had focused her desire upon her father as the primary source of recognition but was met with a rebuffing attitude that left her feeling unseen with no room to question or join except through accommodation. Her lack of mothering had left her with a core feeling of emptiness, at its extreme, a state of "no self." She would relate to others through dependency and compliance, and the world of work seemed unattainable at this time.

As previously mentioned, past defense against a chronic state of yearning and emptiness included overeating, which she eventually overcame with the help of Overeaters Anonymous (OA). In recent years, a physical symptom had developed having to do with severe pain in the hands and lower forearms, a condition which could not be neurologically diagnosed. Psychologically speaking, this suggested that her body was carrying the helpless condition of the "Handless Maiden," an archetypal figure in a fairy tale whose hands are cut off by her father in service to the Devil, leaving the maiden alone and adrift in a world in which she could not grasp or "handle" life. Dee herself referenced another fairy tale, "The Singing Bone," as reflecting the body as instrument of the soul giving expression to psychic pain even after death.

Her last line of defense ultimately was a form of self-destruction in which she would psychologically and physically immobilize herself with an ultra-defiant attitude of "I won't" in the face of an environment which held only a hostile gaze upon her. This stance on the one hand gave expression to her underlying rage, while at the same time kept her safe from retaliation that would accompany overt expression.

The goal of treatment eventually presented itself as the process of an evolving, deeply buried authentic self, achieved through the integration of affects such as depression, rage, fear and shame via a process of differentiating and coming into relationship with them as psychic entities. The subsequent emergence was that of a self, organized around her innate intelligence or mindfulness in service to her imagination. From this position, Dee was eventually able to observe the different, formerly intolerable, parts of herself, as well as the loss of self, associated with periods of descent into the abyss.

In this process dreams occurred highlighting different aspects of the self or different "selves."

1) Initial dream:[2] *She dreamed of being in a spaceship with a male guide. The task at hand was to jump off the ship and land on earth. Dee was apprehensive and the guide went first, then turned back and smiled at her. She took her leap and found herself having landed in a music store on earth.*

Dee's sense of the dream came to be that she felt stuck in space in her life and with her previous analyst. She needed to get some grounding to further her process. The male guide was associated with her new analyst, but more intricately with an inner intuitive guide. The music store brought more associations with her new analyst, but again, more importantly, the idea that she could choose her own tune to dance to. Music also carried associations to the complexity and multiplicity of lines of music all being played at once as an image of the different lines of music at play in her psyche.

During a period of reflection upon her feeling of inferiority with others, Dee dreamed:

> 2) *I am sitting on a lounge chair with two other women to whom I associate the sense of "productive." The back of one had been flayed and blood was flowing into the earth.*

The dream presented a ritual dismemberment in the form of removal of skin as surface and sacrifice to the groundedness of her authentic being indicating that identity of worthlessness was being worked upon from the "backside," i.e., through reflection upon and relationship with her identification with inferiority.

> 3) *An early premonition of the emergence of self-empowerment occurred in a dream in which she found herself in a glade with a marble slab out of which protruded several white pillars of her own height. The one which caught her special attention was the only one colored yellow, a personal special color as well as the alchemical color of sulphureous movement.*

This dream came about during a time of self-reflection related to a dark descent and emotional withdrawal from an unseeing world, thus seeming to symbolize an activation of the underlying potential for a grounded, well-ordered phallic energy specific to herself.

> 4) *During a period of emergent rage associated with a giving over of self to her previous analyst, Dee dreamed she was in a well-lit room with a man who was chained, standing against a wall. There is another person and a leopard in the room. The leopard suddenly charges for the man and tears into his neck and throat. Blood runs all over as the action is repeated again and again. Dee is in terror while the other person is calm as if the event is expected.*

Reflection upon learned helplessness had activated a violently aggressive energy that is the counter to being "gripped by the neck" by her defenses. The aggressive response was something that had been kept at bay and now won't let her go. At the same time, the man chained against the wall, felt like the "handless" aspect of her impotent capacity in the world, with associations to a father and a hapless inner masculinity.

During a period of exploring the distinct quality of her own mind and voice, Dee dreamed the following:

5)

A) *She saw several lions in four rows, equally spaced, looking west at a sunset while standing on their hind legs as if paying respect.*

B) *She is in a room with a group of people and a cage with a large bear inside along with a man. The man throws the bear some meat and departs the cage leaving the door open. The bear gets out of the cage, grasps a woman in its mouth, shakes her, and lets her go. People scream as the bear then goes for a man, then a woman and carries her out of sight around the corner of the cage.*

C) *Dee's head is shaved prior to attending a fund-raising event for "development."*

These dreams are follow-ups of the previous leopard dream marked by alignment and release of primal energy through ritualized events, which indicate the emergence of an empowered self-object as symbolized by the coordinated rows of lions "bearing" witness, and the liberated bear indicated by a re-newed mind and identity as signified by the shaved head.

During the close of this period of gaining a sense of her own ground, Dee dreamed:

6) *She was walking beside a male guide at his insistence on a boardwalk through trees. At the finish of the walk, the guide announces that a walk together had been taken.*

Dee's association was a sense of "walking together, arm in arm" with her grandmother on a path all laid out in the forest. She associated the man with her analyst, as if she had achieved a way of being with her "self" as her own analyst.

Course of Treatment

The course of treatment consisted of a process of separation from the alternately absent/devouring mother and the incorporation of the phallic hand/mind energy of the father. This was accomplished through the careful examination over time of distinct episodes of interaction with family, world and the transference/countertransferential dynamics such that a chaotic internal life could become differentiated and related to as internal objects.

In focusing on the analytic relationship, the narrative of the transference went something like:

I yearn for belonging and reach for my analyst in a dependent mode. He sees my reach but does not gratify me. I see him seeing the reach thereby becoming visible, but not reciprocating in kind, thereby becoming vulnerable to seemingly intolerable affects of rage at him and ensuing shame. He will never see my "wholeness." I withdraw in terror that I am the only one that sees my internal and external reality and therefore, utterly alone. He reaches for me through his inquiry into my state, and I am thrown back on myself. I feel myself rising to meet him but feeling wobbly. Dialogue ensues in which I become steadier, enough to reach for my own mind, but this achievement leaves me with a challenge: be myself and risk being alone, or opt for the comfort of dependency, but loose myself.

The narrative of the analyst's countertransference (related in the first person from this point onwards,) went something like: I feel scrutinized by a vigilant gaze of desire and judgement at the same time. I am wanted, but also being assessed as to whether I will do the right thing and comply. I feel a tension in my stomach, and a force pulling me up out of my normative slouch to the edge of my chair. My curiosity is aroused, and I feel a tingling in my bodily extremities. What I understand as an alternating overt and covert invitation to rescue through merger confronts me, and I am pulled to make *myself* more comfortable by responding in kind. At times, I have done just this through enactments like calling her outside of the session to see if she needed an added session. These gestures on my part only resulted in her confusion and feeling of "creepiness" at the crossing of the boundary. To her consternation I am usually able to resist this pull, and I return her bid with an alternative invitation to inquiry. A sort of tennis match ensues: at first a gentle back and forth, which grows in intensity until I find myself resorting almost exclusively to lobs in return of her slams. Gradually, the nature of the match changes to one in which we are on the same side of the net with me setting her up for her own insights.

Case Process

A vignette of a series of sessions gives a description of process:

Dee had been working on a psychological separation from her devouring internal mother object through interactions with her family and in her work with OA. When an interview for a position as an intern in a clinic with a supervisor who was oblivious and autocratic in the mode of her father went bad, she came to doubt her capabilities and felt perceived shame in the eyes of her analyst. Subsequent sessions focused on repair in this rupture within herself and a sense of renewed self-discovery and empowerment with the realization that she had taken her own ground of perspective in relation to the supervisor. She then reported a dream:

Dee was in a club full of women and girls of all ages, dancing and generally having fun. She then finds herself as a passenger in a car with her father in the driver's seat. He grabs her hand and puts it upon his penis. She pulls it back and cries, "No, no!" He replies, "What do you expect—dancing, pressing things against me, and taking

your panties off !" She responds by throwing a potato at
her father.

Dee related to the dream with mixed feelings of concern and pleasure. The dream ego (Dee) had been frightened but strangely ambivalent at the episode with her father but had taken real pleasure in the festive event with the women. She talked about seeing the two parts of the dream as connected, in that psychologically she had been moving toward becoming her own woman as she has taken in hand the phallic power she had attributed to her father/ analyst. The exchange between herself and father/analyst indicates the resistance that she has unconsciously held in relation to this development—taking on her own authority had been associated with becoming like her father. She associated her final gesture to her connection with the primal phallus and weaponizing the "root" from her grounded psyche.

Subsequent sessions focused on Dee's relationship to me as a parallel to her relationship with her father. From this position, she expected that I had "answers" just like her father held answers, knowledge of which she was denied, and did not even have the right to request without a backlash of shame. As a result, she was left unseen and without value. The internal father and internal analyst were both represented in the breakthrough imaged by the dream father's relinquishing access to his penis, but only in a manner which conveyed shame while gratifying himself. Again, the double bind, she could hold power, but only with shame. The psychological effect of this backlash came to the patient through the appearance of several bodily symptoms related to her female organs and hands. In response to these, she took a stand of "I won't," resisting acquiescing to father/doctor/analyst by means of refusing to see a medical doctor for her condition.

During this period another dream appeared:

Dee is walking down a dirt road to meet her father. She
reaches the meeting place at the end of the road, but he is
not there. She turns and sees a tree, not fully grown and
appearing as if near death. It is leaning, pointing back
down the road from which she came. She starts back and

*the tree slides along the ground as if following her and
calling for help.*

Although in the dream Dee had little emotional reaction to the
absent father, in associating to the dream she was quite surprised,
especially after the last dream when she was in the car with her
father. She was quite taken with the idea of the absence of her
father. She noted the end of the road with father's absence and the
turning point imaged in the dream as significant in her process.
She associated the tree with its connection through roots and the
idea of inter-species care, and noted that the tree was pointing out
the next direction, back to from where she came. An association
took her to the memory of a sand play image she had previously
created of a girl sitting alone on a stump of a tree (diminished
father/phallic energy,) with the stump acting as protection, as
well as an association to herself as a girl finding comfort in a
small Christmas tree. Another perspective would see the tree as
derivative of the perpetrating internal father object present in the
last dream who now could only meet her as a dying tree, albeit
pointing the way back as if towards her own ground of being.
Toward the end of the session, she became tearful, and I inquired
as to what the tears might be saying.

Dee had been unable to answer and between sessions the
question worked upon her in a negative way. She took it as an
indication of my disapproval for crying, resulting in a wave of
shame and a descent into a psychological abyss, toned with a
defiant sense of "I won't" relative to the care of doctors and myself.
In the following session, she was able to articulate that her tears
were for her own struggle of the last twenty years to find herself,
a struggle which she connected with the girl on the stump and
the girl with the Christmas tree. She was also able to observe that
her withdrawing defiance, relative to doctor care for her physical
symptoms, was an attempt to make herself matter in response to
a perceived unseeing eye from me.

In the next session, feeling the pull to reach out to her, I
responded to her opening request for my feedback and perspective
by spending most of the session laying out a psychological

picture of what I saw happening sequentially in our sessions in terms of the parallel of the dynamics in her relationship with her father, with me and with the doctors, and with the movement that was taking place in those relationships. Although I thought we had worked long enough and in tandem enough with these issues, I eventually came to see this intervention on my part as an enactment, discharging my own anxiety in the face of her need for a secure hand. The following session I found out how off base I was with the "knowing" intervention. Dee opened the session by asking me for more information and then withdrawing emotionally when I responded defensively that I thought I had laid it all out and really had nothing more beneficial to offer. The session was spent in an agonizing standoff with Dee in withdrawn despair, and I, left feeling helpless, without hands to reach her.

In the subsequent session, we were able to process what had happened: when Dee's request was gratified by me, she felt held as if being "cradled." When I didn't expand on it, she felt abandoned, humiliated and shamed; I was punishing her by withholding. From the standpoint of her unconscious, I had held out the penis and then punished her for this gesture while gratifying myself. Inevitably, we had enacted the dynamic expressed in the dream with her father in the car. In this session, she was able to experience herself as utilizing her observing psychological eye and mind in conjunction with me to co-create the narrative of the enactment as an object for reflection.

Following this session, Dee had a dream:

She was with her own mother and was taking care of her mother's mother. The grandmother was alone in a hospital room, doing better, and wearing a red and green plaid jacket with a maroon shirt underneath which Dee associated with the little Christmas tree which gave her such comfort as a girl.

When Dee woke up, she felt resolved and started calling doctors to tend to her symptoms. In the next session, she reported the dream and talked about her grandmother as a cold, rigid woman, who had stayed with the family when the grandfather had been hospitalized in a mental hospital in response to his uncontrollably violent behavior (he had sexually abused his daughter, Dee's mother.) A multigenerational, psychological mother-daughter reparative process was occurring.

Apparently, the previous session, in which I had acknowledged my enactment as a complex discharge of my own anxiety in reaction to her need—was reparative. We could again piece together the session as a co-created event with meaning. The connection of girl with Christmas tree had enabled Dee to connect with the holding power which she yearned for from me within herself in the form of grandma's red and green plaid Christmas jacket. The maternal holding instinct, which had been missing in the previous two generations, had been discovered in Dee's unconscious, and she was then able to take care of herself by giving herself over to medical authorities.

A later illustration of the chaotic field of transference/countertransference subsequently occurred in a tough session of dialogue regarding Dee's despair over not feeling as if she was progressing adequately. Her need was for certainty or "answers" to hold onto, rather than dealing with the more elliptical, fluid nature of her experience of the analytic process. Toward the end of the session, she came to a point of resolution in herself and made a statement expressing where she had come to. Her statement was followed by the sound of a dog barking, and she teared up. She then looked closely at me and asked if I knew what her tears were about.

I was taken aback, and said I didn't have a clue with a somewhat severe and defensive tone, feeling like I was again being placed in the position of "authority," who didn't have an answer I was supposed to have. She took my response as a put down; I had "thrown her against the wall" (like the man chained to the wall in her previous dream.) However, this time she was able to came back at me with her response to her own question (like the leopard at the neck of the chained man in the previous dream.) The dog's bark was an indication to her of a connection with the world, which in turn, signified that she held "meaning" within herself. She had asked the question, not reaching for my hand in answer, but reasonably thinking that I would be able to know that she knew what was going on based on similar past occurrences. I had been caught off guard, and in my obtuseness, had enacted a defensive response in which I had pushed her away, but she was now able to re-cover herself spontaneously.

In conclusion, the following ideas emerged from this case:

1) The analytic process makes its way through the mutual inter-relation of patient and analyst.

2) This interaction will inevitably bring pressure to bear on the analyst to relieve the patient of the pain involved in the patient's internal psychological structuring. To give in to this pressure will enact a response within the patient wherein intolerable feelings will be split off, resulting in a dualistic psychological state.

3) When this happens, the *opus contra naturum*, or resistance to what seems natural as an impulse, will enable a holding of psychological tension such that the psyche of the patient is enabled to metabolize its own form and experience itself in a "whole" or nondualist way—the process Jung saw as the autonomous self healing movement of the psyche toward its true form.

Out of the Swamp emerges the Matter . . .

Endnotes

[1] A version of this chapter, as case presentation by the author, appeared in a series of videos produced by the Friends of Jung of Washington D.C., as an introduction to the basic tenets of Jungian Psychology.

[2] Often the initial dream of the analysis, a dream that occurs around the time of first contact or first session, has special significance foreshadowing the direction of the analytic process.

Chapter 10

Psychopathology I: A Double Vision

The Matrix and Meaning of Character: An Archetypal and Developmental Approach,[1] a book written by Nancy Dougherty and Jacqueline West, as the length of the title suggests, covers a lot of ground in its quest to delineate and describe developmental and archetypal approaches to psychopathology. The word matrix comes from the Latin term for breeding animals and is etymologically related to the word "mater" or "mother." It refers to: 1) an enveloping substance within which something else originates, or 2) a mold or die. In other words, a matrix is something encompassing consciousness and man-made, an expression of the dual nature of the psyche—personal and "larger than." Meaning as a word, carries a dynamic quality, something intended, signified. Literally, it is something carried from one place to another, a crossing over. If "matrix" is fixed, matter, boundary, category, static, "meaning" is movement toward an end, spirit, transcendent, multiple, fluid. The alchemical purpose here is to bring mercury to the lead, an enlivening *anima*, Isis to the dead matter of Osiris, moisture to dry clinical language and concept, while at the same time giving earth or ground to abstract meaning. Alchemy: make the fixed volatile and the volatile fixed.

Multiple layers are embedded in the word "character." Etymologically, it contains the Greek root "to engrave," as well as the Latin root for "original" or "distinct." From this foundation, emerges a paradox—that which is essentially engraved (manmade) serves both a defensive function and an archetypal (transpersonal) intention. Individuation occurs through a distinct mode of being, a character structure. It is through our woundedness, in conjunction with its archetypal background, that we can access our deepest and most uniquely creative energies. Character is not just psychopathology, but personality—all of us, therapist and patient alike, each individuality "engraved" in character. When analysts allow themselves to see these structures as patterns that underlie their own character, they find that they work with patients in a field of mutuality, in contrast to a field of hierarchical distance in which there is the knower and the known. Here, psychological thought is at once both theory of personality and of psychopathology, just as Freud and Jung meant for it to be.

Character has been a staple orientation of traditional psychoanalytic thinking since Freud, whose conceptualization of the term evolved throughout the course of his thinking regarding the development of personality. In psychoanalysis, the term refers to the enduring, patterned functioning of an individual, his or her habitual way of thinking, feeling, and acting. From a psychodynamic standpoint, it is the person's customary way of reconciling internal conflict. Character is made up of an integrated constellation of traits which are stable and ego-syntonic, as opposed to the ego-dystonic quality of neurotic symptoms. It was Freud's struggle with the transference resistance of his patients that led him to orient his focus toward the workings of the ego and the evolution of character. Through character structure, one gains satisfaction and achievement in life, but an exaggeration or inflexibility in the structure ultimately causes psychic pain, making the individual amenable for treatment.

"An Archetypal and Developmental Approach"—the authors are attempting to alchemically congeal two ways of seeing that have traditionally divided—both Freudian from Jungian, and within the Jungian schools—symbolic from developmental approaches to the psyche. Archetypal and developmental, transcendent and historical, intentional and regressive—can't have the warp without the woof the authors propose, to which their weaving provides evidence. The value in presenting the two approaches together is that while the developmental approach is necessary to tease out personal complexes and as an enactment of the archetypal healing ritual of returning to origins by exploring the psychological reality of reliving the past in the present, the archetypal approach offers the big picture, maps of universal structures, as informing this venture.

The final phrase, "Searching for the Wellsprings of Spirit:" by making spirit a matter of the wellspring, that is, depth, below the surface, the authors go against the classical notion of spiritual home in the heavens, and they maintain a psychological stance which synthesizes opposites—above and below, spirit and matter. Memory is etymologically associated with the well, and thus the overall purpose of the book: "to enliven the body of knowledge about character structures by remembering the mythological themes that underlie human development."[2]

Mainstream clinical traditions in depth psychology are followed by the authors as they establish their psychological bearings in the system of ego development as a process of differentiation. The three particular developmental phases they differentiate—primal, narcissistic, and pre-neurotic—are "narratives" telling the story of character structure emerging through the interweaving of age-specific factors and individual specific relational patterns. The authors utilize the dominating concept in traditional Jungian developmental theory, the "ego-Self axis," as a metaphor depicting the tension between the emergent worldly ego and the transcendent individual essence, the Self. The Self is not depicted as a reified structure, but a process, "an objective reality that weaves universal meaning into subjective, personal reality."[3]

The primal phase refers to the first eighteen months of life. The task during this phase is for the infant to emerge from a relatively unformed state to one of separateness and cohesiveness, the consolidation of differentiation, ego evolving. Relational patterns formed in the primal phase create individual character structures along a continuum ranging from flexible, healthy expansion of the ego to fixed, pathological defense patterns of withdrawal, splitting, and projective identification resulting in the constriction of the ego. In other words, within each character structure there is a continuum from health to pathology.[4]

The defensive nature of the primal phase is seen as a platform upon which to construct the notion of the schizoid character. "A defense begins as a healthy, creative adaptation and earns the term 'defense' only when it is employed repetitively and inflexibly in the face of an unmanageable threat."[5] In the authors' conceptualizations, relational patterns of seeking, withdrawing, and antagonizing may be used adaptively, but may come to be more fixed into a defensive structure depending upon the experienced threat. The early diseased personality is based fundamentally on defense formation, leaving little space for emergent capacities, for qualities such as joy or aloneness and overwhelming evolving psychomotor structures. In all three-character structures in the primal phase, an underdeveloped ego and subsequent defended character structure impede the purposeful flow of psychic energy along the ego-Self axis, a dynamic which is ultimately in service to the central concern of the primal phase, a basic struggle for survival. What is pertinent for the authors' overall, unifying theoretical orientation is their emphasis on the psychodynamic defense formation in the primal phase as reflecting archetypal forms.

The "narcissistic phase," between eighteen and thirty months, closely follows the thinking of Austrian psychoanalyst, Heinz Kohut, in its emphasis on the presence of "mirroring" as a key element in the child's ability to navigate the evolving space between itself and the parenting figures. Following object-relations theory, the pre-neurotic stage is the period from two and a half to four years, when the child is extracting its identity from a dyadic foundation but still hasn't attained the Oedipal struggle. In the pre-neurotic phase, the defenses of repression, rationalization, undoing, turning against oneself, compartmentalization, and displacement are utilized both adaptively and defensively.

The above three historical developmental stages are venues for the enactment of three distinct relational patterns, withdrawing, seeking, and antagonistic. Withdrawing is a habitual pulling away from contact with others, while seeking is a customary movement toward relationship. The pathological extremes of these behaviors result in either shell-like or merging patterns respectively. The antagonistic pattern is based on a kind of predatory behavior that can take the extreme of a hostile attitude toward self and others. Each of the three relational patterns finds a home in each of the developmental phases.

Although they are presenting a model of categories for individual identity, the authors also offer cautionary disclaimers regarding the intellectual danger of fitting individuals into categorical boxes. "We encourage you to utilize these concepts symbolically, playfully even. Hold them lightly in your mind."[6] In addition, the authors pointedly emphasize the need for self-diagnosis on the part of clinicians. They recognize the field between analyst and patient as bipolar, inter-subjectival, "requiring the analyst to be thoroughly familiar with her own character structure, including her regressive challenges and shadow dynamics."[7] With this sensibility, the notion of matrix now comes to encompass both analyst and patient at once. In sum, the authors' diagnostic intentions are ultimately in service to the archetypal tradition of calling out the names of each region of the underworld as a psychological necessity in the exploration of pathological life.

It is the goal of the authors to indicate how psychopathology needs to be understood with a view to the interrelationship of developmental and archetypal factors. In keeping with the sense that it is narratives of archetypal schemes in their stark form that are helpful in the depiction of psychopathology as the opening into the strange structuring of underlying character forms, the authors turn to fairy tales and myths. I would suggest that these stories are crucial for the understanding of psychopathology because they present images which are the primary signifiers, or language, of the psyche, and because story allows for entrance into the *experience* of pathology by both patient and doctor.

Myths and fairy tales present narratives, which universally express the primary structures of the psyche in images which in themselves hold meaning particular to the world they are expressing. Archetypal images represent ways of being, seeing, and acting that tend to be similar in certain situations across cultures and throughout the ages. They are universal metaphors indicating in a starkly imagistic way the patterns of how things are in their bare, psychological grounding. Each image represents a world in which consciousness finds itself given certain contexts. In themselves, archetypes do not have positive or negative poles of dark and light; they simply are. Archetypes are not pathological in themselves, rather they are at the core of experience that presents itself through pathology. It was Jung's insight to see the hierarchy—gods in disease, in theory, in conceptual structure, and in the complex—not the other way around. Archetypal figures don't have issues; they *are* the issue. Oedipus cannot be diagnosed as having a complex; he *is* the complex. Most importantly, stories present phenomena within *context* so that analytic focus does not get fixated on one agency or cause-effect dynamics, but enables a perspective that sees phenomena as an emergence appearing out of the interaction of multiple agencies.

Withdrawing Pattern

Schizoid—Little Match Girl

From the standpoint of ego development, within the withdrawing pattern composed of three phases, the schizoid character structure appears in the primal phase. In other words, the presence of an absence is the touchstone of the schizoid character, and persistence in the face of swirling abandonment is the key for treatment. The schizoid person can be seen in a paradoxical way—on the one hand, habitually declining to engage with the stimulation of the external world in favor of a level of "archaic and rich imagery" in the inner world. At the same time, at its deeper levels, the inner world itself "is imaged and experienced as a *void* . . . a vast hollow space, uninhabited by any life form."[8] Caught between the threat of the external world and the wasteland of the void that is sensed underneath, "these patients may suffer pervasive bodily fears of disintegration: fears of vanishing into nothingness, coming apart in thin air, decaying into compost."[9]

The authors present Hans Christian Andersen's fairy tale, "The Little Match Girl," as reflecting and amplifying the schizoid character structure.

> A motherless girl, selling matches on a street in mid-winter, bare of foot and hand, sans sales or food, terrified by father in a cold home, with the coming of night, sits in the snow, burns all of her wares, and dies in the grip of a fantasy of joining her grandmother in the heavens.

From the ego-orientation of the authors, the Match Girl is given a developmental history, assigned inner psychodynamics, and assessed as maladaptive. She does not suffer shame or guilt, rather the severe lack of mothering attachment results in a life experience of perpetual threat. The girl is deeply withdrawn, paralyzed, and unable to reach out for help. Her lack of connection to others and withdrawal cause her to succumb to the cold embrace of death.

In contrast, a view from the standpoint of the archetypal image itself would see in the tale an atmosphere of the *senex*: the old man, cold and alone, isolated and empty, paradoxically finding his place in an abandoned girl, an indication that archetypes don't recognize gender or age. It would see the story being not about the lack of development or capacity but about the presence of something else—lack, absence, *nigredo*, darkness, death, aloneness—ritualized in the burning off of the matches as the diminishing spark of life. Following Jung's sense that all consciousness is a product of fantasy, that is, the everyday world created through an image, this vein of interpretation would hold that the Match Girl *is* the archetypal reality of aloneness. Her image prefigures the characters of Samuel Beckett in establishing isolation and desolation as a predominant form of being, and Jack London's lone traveler systematically undermining the fire he was attempting to build in the Arctic cold in the story "To Build a Fire." From this perspective, it would not be that the girl cannot reach out for help, but rather that she reaches out when, as with another withdrawing figure, Emily Dickinson, "Death / . . . kindly stopped for me."

The authors utilize the notion of differentiation to indicate a process of separation of conscious from unconscious in service of ego development. The archetypalist might share this term by pointing to the differentiation that can occur within the archetypal image itself. What is helpful from the standpoint of an integrated clinical approach is the authors' ability to see a tale within the various psychoanalytic theories regarding the schizoid condition. As well, they use story to indicate intersubjective features in the analytic dyad such that there ". . . can be freezing in the midst of plenty, looking at life through a frosted windowpane, without the ability to reach out and ask for warmth . . ."[10] within the analytic situation itself.

The Seeking Pattern

Dependent Narcissistic Structure—Ophelia, Mother Holle, Demeter/Persephone

Within the seeking pattern the dependent narcissistic character appears in the narcissistic phase and is especially significant given the cultural overlay of its symptomatology. Who does not want the individual dedicated to hard work serving upon organizational committees and in official capacities year after year, the romantic dedicated to the relationship, or the inspiring teacher? Yet, the authors show us through vivid description of developmental dynamics, archetypal amplification, and case studies of how a particular pathos underlies these seemingly attractive behaviors. They make the subtle distinction between the dependent personality disorder and the dependent narcissistic character structure by noting that whereas the former tends to cling out of a need to be taken care of, the latter's underlying intention is to gain the recognizing, approving, loving gaze of other people. "Her concern is more deeply rooted in an inner sense that the source of love and meaning lies in the other."[11] While others experience the person as self-sacrificing, the narcissistic dynamics of idealizing/devaluing others and aggrandizing/diminishing self, underlie the seemingly desirable behavior. "Whether apparently 'giving' or 'getting,' he is forever . . . insatiably hungry but also psychically impenetrable."[12]

Corresponding archetypal images are illustrative of what the authors are getting at. The Cinderella figure in the Mother Holle fairy tale serves a deeper intention of "the search" in her journey into the underworld. The wandering of Demeter in her grief and Persephone's descent in joining Hades depict seeking as the painful widening and deepening of overly familiar dimensions. The authors' use of Mary Pipher's interpretation of Ophelia as a dependent character holding ". . . no inner direction . . . her value . . . experienced solely through the approval of her father and Hamlet . . ." however, is problematic.[13] Here, Pipher is mistakenly placing a contemporary ego-oriented perspective inside a classical dramatic character with universal qualities. Shakespeare's female characters are characteristically strong in comparison to their male counterparts in that they know more of who they are, what they want, and what is called for in the larger picture. Ophelia's love for her father and brother, and especially for Hamlet, is a selfless love which runs up against obtuse (father), ego-identified (brother), and self-oriented (Hamlet) objects. Her "madness" is the only means of authentic expression available to her in an unreceptive, uncomprehending environment and death is a sacrifice reflecting the deep corruption and hopelessness of love in her world.

The authors' analytic work in the case of Paul is exceptionally admirable. The study is presented under the overarching warning of the danger of the unknowing analyst falling prey to his or her own narcissistic tendencies by becoming caught in the patient's inflation/deflation, cocreating a mutual world of self-involvement. Here, we get a good sense of the analyst's experience and its reflection of the analytic third world. "[H]e constantly aimed to get something from me, something he then paradoxically could not allow in. It frequently felt like we'd do the same futile exercise over and over. At these moments, it seemed as if our work had become simply another round of his endless sucking. I felt 'used' and discarded."[14]

The Antagonistic Pattern

Psychopathic Character Structure—"The Sea Hare" and the Trickster

Within the antagonistic pattern at the primal phase lies the psychopathic character, and the authors start with the contemporary cultural fascination with psychopathy. Indeed, this is the place to start, and this idea could stand in-depth scrutiny. As ingrained and pervasive as it is in a capitalistic culture oriented toward competition and power, psychopathy can be considered less a pathology than a way of life, ultimately revealing itself in the psychopathy of its elected leadership, The authors' implication of the media as source ("we are being desensitized and presented with compelling models of violence"[15]) lies in contrast to alternative viewpoints that 1) fantasy and action in the world are not the same, and 2) cultural images are reflections of the collective psyche in its essence, that is, the media reflects, not determines, who we are.

A thorough review of the literature leads to an encapsulating summary of the condition. "[A] psychopathically structured person is someone who suffered a massive failure of human attachment and, as a result, has been unable to incorporate objects into their inner world. Subsequently, this person insists upon and relies on omnipotent control over others."[16] The hallmark of the psychopath is an inability to relate to others except as external objects available to control. The psychopath places his condition of lack at the feet of society as ultimately responsible and acts it out irremediably and unreflectively in a vain attempt at its completion. The ego of the future psychopath in the first nine months of life, unable to overcome stranger anxiety and denied the opportunity for superego development, identifies with aggression itself or the predator, and the budding personality is unable to form attachments to others. A very helpful clinical vignette indicates the pitfalls for the therapist treating psychopathy in a naive manner, unrelated to the anger that psychopathy inevitably evokes in the therapist. A good diagnostic indicator is simply finding oneself not liking a patient and not knowing why, and the authors indicate that the paradoxical key ingredient to treating a psychopath is to have no investment in change.

Dougherty and West are particularly good in this chapter in reviewing countertransference challenges and in describing pitfalls from their own work, which elucidate the subjectivity of the analyst entrapped in the web of the psychopathic structure. They carry their sensibility regarding the countertransference over into the archetypal realm by bringing in the fairy tale of "The Sea Hare" and by introducing the mythical Trickster into their dialogue. "The Sea Hare" is the story of a haughty, heavily defended princess, who lives on her aggression in the sense that she habitually attracts and then beheads her suitors. Her counterpart is a youngest brother, who eventually wins her over with the help of various animal/divinities, particularly those of the trickster, shape-shifter. The creative stroke by the authors is to analyze the tale by inserting the analyst as the wooing counterpart to the patient as defended hostile princess and emphasizing the need for the analyst to be able to take on different "shapes" in the underlying analytic dialogue while constantly aware of his/her own unconscious process in relation to the patient.

With their analysis of the psychopathic character structure, the authors have woven three interrelating strands of their discourse in a highly successful manner: a review of theory to come up with a compact but complete image of the structure and dynamics of the condition, a descriptive narration of a case study focusing on the countertransference, and an elaboration of the countertransference process through an analysis of its archetypal mirror in fairy tale and myth.

Alpha Narcissistic Structure

"Mirror, Mirror, on the Wall," Princess Thrushbeard, and Medea

The authors find the alpha narcissist within the antagonistic pattern at the narcissistic phase. The touchstone of the alpha narcissistic structure is the desperate need to stay on top while feeling constantly under siege. The alpha narcissist is constantly rejecting and ridiculing while defending through alternate idealizing and devaluing in a never-ending effort to be at the top of a self-created hierarchy. The authors include a very informative discussion of the role of envy, making distinctions among the various forms of narcissism. "The dependent narcissist tends to agonize over her envious feelings . . . the counter-dependent narcissist denies her envy . . . the alpha narcissistic person acts it out antagonistically."[17] The authors reference the dark queen in "Little Snow White" perpetually seeking reassurance from the magic mirror as to who is the fairest of all. The question and the mirror in turn can be seen as a reflection of the world mirror from which the psyche seeks identity. There is never a moment of consciousness without an envious desiring. The work of Melanie Klein and Otto Kernberg is referenced as focusing upon the infant's attack upon the good object by entering it and spoiling its contents as a primitive defense for the purpose of preserving omnipotence and grandiosity. The alpha narcissist lives under constant pressure to triumph but can never allow feelings of success. What he or she yearns for but can't be allowed, achievement or success, is not to be available for others, and relationships take place through denigration and contempt. The relevant fairy-tale image is that of the princess in the opening of the tale "King Thrushbeard." From the standpoint of ego development, a princess,. beautiful yet proud, neurotically maintains herself by inviting and then rejecting various suitors with accompanying ridicule. On the other hand, taking the princess as an archetypal image reveals that it is her energy that allows women (and men) to say "No" when they need to.

The mythical amplification focuses on Medea, known best for the terror of her manipulations and vengeful wrath, but a closer look gives a more complex picture. Medea's name, like that of the Gorgon, Medusa, has its roots in the Sanskrit concept of *medha* or female wisdom. She was a sorceress known for the art of healing—her name related to the word "medicine," and she had the power to raise the dead. Her commitment to her husband, Jason, was exhibited in providing him with a drug and advice, which allowed him to accomplish "heroic" deeds. It was she, not Jason, who stole the Golden Fleece that Jason sought and then enabled his escape by murdering and dismembering her brother so that her father was distracted from pursuit. Years later, she had had enough of Jason and killed a female rival for her husband's favors with a garment that burned her victim to death and then slayed her own two children by Jason in response to his abandonment of her.

If we are to understand the archetypal energy embodied in Medea, we need to view the context in which her actions take place. Medea has a special power relative to women, and she calls upon divinities of feminine power to back her—stern, sharp shooting Artemis of the hunt and Artemis' cousin, Hekate, who holds the key to the underworld. Her case is solid from the background of feminine consciousness—after enabling Jason's triumphs, he betrays her, and Medea makes clear, "touch her (woman's) right in marriage, and there's no bloodier spirit."[18] The chorus echoes, "The fiercest anger of all, the most incurable, is that which rages in the place of dearest love."[19] This particular rage will not rest until it finds a valued victim, giving us an indication of how, from an archetypal perspective, violence finds its home in domestic space, but there is a cost. What Medea has lost is a husband and children, but more so, that which lies deepest in the psyche: need for homeland. "Of all pains and hardships none is worse / Than to be deprived of your native land."[20]

Finally, we see that Medea archetypal energy, which the authors associate with the narcissistic character, is evoked in the context of severe wounding, which seeks its own redemption. The self-healing function of the psyche will choose images of figures representing nothing but raw power to indicate a self-empowerment process taking place. Dreams of individuals with low self-worth will depict the dreamer sleeping with power mongers, wearing the leather jacket of a Mafioso, meeting up with a mass murderer, or killing off babies as an indication that a movement toward power is happening with an intensity counter to the ego's fierce resistance to sELF-enhancement.

This section contains another description of the transfernce/countertranference issues in working with patients of this type, and the need for accurate assessment and diagnosis to avoid a superficial kind of therapy that ultimately colludes with the patient's pathology. The authors present the key as an analytic frame governed by the shape-shifting shaman, or trickster, that allows for both the patient's idealizing, devaluing, and annihilating projections onto the analyst and an accompanying regression to the underlying paranoid place. "Regression into paranoia puts a person with an alpha character structure into a position to experience and integrate a . . . potential for vulnerability and anxiety."[21] The vicissitudes of working with such a patient in analysis are described in detail:

> "I often felt exhausted, frustrated, and angry. Yet I also sometimes wondered if her terrible suffering was somehow my fault . . . 'one's essential identity as a helper is being eradicated.' I was afraid to confront Elizabeth . . . afraid to contribute more to her sense of internal devastation, afraid of the hatred she directed towards me, afraid of her intelligent rationalizations, afraid of her acting out. I . . . felt that my hands were tied . . . [but as] I was doing worse, she seemed to be doing somewhat better."[22]

Ultimately, the bipolar field of swirling antagonism and feelings of inferiority brought out a judicious aggresion in the analyst, allowing the therapy to move to a different, more refined, but equally difficult phase.

Passive-aggressive Character Structure—Tar Baby/Trickster

The pre-neurotic phase is represented within the antagonistic pattern by the passive-aggressive type of personality. Inevitably, in a culture where dominance plays such a strong part, the "other side" finds its expression, and there is no better image of passive aggression than the inevitable Tar Baby. With this character, the more one aggresses, the less dominant one becomes. The trademark for passive aggression is underlying defeat and inferiority with accompanying envy and underlying rage, all defended with rationalization and denial. From the psychodynamic standpoint, the passive aggressive character structure is formed at the pre-neurotic, oral and anal stages, as a compromise formation. Aggressive impulses are countered by guilt, engendering feelings of envy, ambivalence regarding relationships, deep hostility, set up inefficiencies, seduction coupled with perpetual dissatisfaction, and the tendency to externalize blame. Common behavior patterns include gas lighting, baiting and switching, denial, and denigration of others' efforts and successes. The authors feel that connection is the overriding goal of treatment, and finding disguised aggression is the primary therapeutic intention.

I would submit that the story of the Tar Baby allows for a widening of context for assessment. In the ageless Uncle Remus Tale, Tar Baby is set up as a trap for Rabbit by Fox, who jealous of Rabbit's high self-regard, fashions a doll of tar for Rabbit to get stuck in—the mess of the passive-aggressive psyche thinly disguised by seductive come-on—a classic Trickster move. Captured by Fox and Bear, Rabbit, the Trickster *par excellance*, turns the tables on his captors by inducing them to throw him into the Briar Patch, which seemingly torturous, is actually his home turf. "Oh, please Br'er Bear, Br'er Fox, do with me whatever you want, but please, oh please, don't throw me into that Briar Patch!" Sure enough, into the Briar Patch he is thrown, and off he goes on another adventure. One trick outdoes another, and from the standpoint of ego development, little might be seen as gained. . . but going on to the next round of tricks *is* the Trickster process, and each time around, there is a differentiation, something else particular emerges, and that is the creative energy of the Trickster at work.

As with the other sections on the antagonistic modes of relating, the countertransference process is described remarkably well, with the warning, "the therapist may have to wrestle diligently with her own early wounds in order not to get entrapped by the patient's myriad obstructions, swipes, silences, etc. Effectively *receiving and metabolizing* thoroughly denied aggression is without doubt a sophisticated art."[23] ["T]hese well-developed intuitions of mine were neither appreciated by nor useful to Paul . . . it was with quiet reserve that I sat with my own frustration . . . (ultimately giving up conscious therapeutic intention) I then took it upon myself to live with this sadness and leave Paul to his individual form of development . . . We need not suppose that this person must develop conscious insight and effective integration of affect . . . Paul's growth happened without insight."[24]

The overall thesis of Daugherty and West is that individuation is not an abstract or reified process but occurs through particular structures. They give an account of how each structural form may be determined psychodynamically, therapeutically addressed, and how the particular psychological space can be animated with archetypal imagery, which encompasses the analytic space affecting therapist and patient alike.

It is important to remember, as the authors do, that in its original sense, the "engraving" of character is a unique, individual essence, which resists categorization or systemization. Systems are not of substance in themselves but artifacts that emerge from archetypal fantasies. Jung posited a way of knowing that embraces a third order paradoxically between and embracing developmental psychodynamics and archetypal orientation—through image or *esse in anima*. In the next and final chapter, we shall track the evolution of a different sense of psychopathology through this third order.

Out of the Matter emerges the Work . . .

Endnotes

[1] The author is grateful to Dougherty and West for the opportunity to review their book. The review and their thorough response is published in *Spring 88*, Winter 2012, Spring Journal.

[2] Dougherty, N. and West, J., *The Matrix and Meaning of Character*, p. 1.

[3] *Ibid*, p. 7.

[4] See next chapter for Freud's similar vision in *The Problem of Anxiety*.

[5] Dougherty and West, p. 9

[6] *Ibid*, p. 13.

[7] *Ibid*, p. 16.

[8] *Ibid*, p. 27.

[9] *Ibid*, p. 27.

[10] *Ibid*, p. 39.

[11] *Ibid*, p. 135.

[12] *Ibid*, p. 136.

[13] *Ibid*, p. 134.

[14] *Ibid*, p. 147.

[15] *Ibid*, p. 181.

[16] *Ibid*, p. 186.

[17] *Ibid*, p. 213.

[18] Euripides, "Medea" in *Medea and Other Plays*, p. 25.

[19] *Ibid*, p. 32.

[20] *Ibid*, p. 37.

[21] Dougherty and West, p. 230.

[22] *Ibid*, p. 224.

[23] *Ibid*, p. 255.

[24] *Ibid*, p. 252-3.

Chapter Eleven

Psychopathology II: Soul as Borderline

> The soul has its own logos, which increases itself.
> — Heraclitus

In 1956, a gifted student of modern English philosophy and Jungian psychology at age 33, was killed in an auto accident. In the wreckage of the car was found a manuscript of a three quarters completed work. The book, *The Logos of the Soul*, edited and published in 1963 by James Hillman for whom it was something of an inspiration, was an attempt to integrate two seemingly distinct orders of understanding: philosophy and its use of concept and science in its discipline of observation, in staking out a separate epistemological ground for psychology as a "study of the mind." The author was Evangelou Christou, and his work emphasized the need for a structure of principles for depth psychology, distinct from body (matter) and mind (spirit) but encompassing aspects of each—a logic or science of the soul as an empirical agent.

In tracing strands at the roots of psychoanalysis, we have been following what seems to be a universal notion of the relationship of two larger-than-life agencies: Disorder (*khaos*) and Order (*ananke*), with the former being the starting point, and the forces of the latter being marshaled for eventual triumph. We have seen how this narrative has come to play in the universal process of healing, but have also taken note of how, in the complexities of this event, there exists a fundamental interrelationship between the two, a third order of being. Different healing modalities make this part of the account depending on the particular *ethos* of the culture, but it would be for psychoanalysis to take this interactive or ambivalent sensibility to an extreme in the execution of the "analytic attitude." Christou's little-known but provocative thinking introduces the history of psychoanalysis as a struggle of different voices to give expression to a paradoxical third order in service to healing. In this way, we can conclude our exploration with an extension of the notion of psychopathology, as well as a sense of the challenges implied in the previous chapters for an understanding of psychological life that is authentic to the psyche.

Christou followed his teacher, Ludwig Wittgenstein, who proposed that the problem in philosophy was its use of language, which tends toward abstraction leaving out the ground of everyday experience. For Wittgenstein, language was a matter of a game, and the need was to use it in reference to actual context, not metaphysical signification of meaning. The problem with science, on the other hand, was its reliance on technique of detached observation and measurement as a means of ascertaining objective reality leaving out the belief system, the philosophy, that underlies method. Christou's notion was that psychology could have a place in the historical milieu of science and philosophy in that neither can give *soul* a "reality" in the way an expansive imagination of principles in philosophy and science could do according to his vision of psychology.[1]

Here, Christou follows Jung's distinction between *esse in ra*, rational being related to the tangible world, *aesse in intellectu*, the world as perceived through concept, and a third world, *esse in anima*, the reality of lived life or being through soul.[2]

"Living reality is the product neither of the actual, objective behavior of things nor of the formulated idea exclusively, but rather of the combination of both in the living psychological process."[3]

When privileging an aesthetic mode (in contrast to material or spiritual) as the "logic" of the psyche, an aesthetically integrating expression is necessary. Jung ultimately found this in his alchemical studies when he extended his sense of symbol to imagination as the fundamental mode of the psyche.[4] Imagination, for Jung, was the agency through which images are formed, and it is in image as world that consciousness, meaning and being, dwell. "We live immediately only in the world of images."[5] Jung was positing another way of knowing in addition to the rational or ordering mode: through image, or *esse in anima*. From this perspective, "image and meaning are identical."[6] In other words, we don't need systems to be logical; each image holds its own logic within the world we live in at every moment expressed and experienced through image. "Concepts are coined and negotiable values; images are life."[7]

Christou was phenomenological in that he wanted to emphasize the unique experience of the individual "personality" as the proper ground of meaning for depth psychology, lived life as the "fact" to be studied, the description of which would be "evidence" in lieu of the detached observations of science and the abstract concepts of philosophy. The degree to which the description of experience fits into patterns of collective experience, the public reality, would serve as "validation," the appropriate expression of which would be found in the arts, drama, and ritual. Christou's insistence was that meaning exists in experience, not through that constructed by the ego, but through the reverberations of universality in the context of everyday life.

For Jung, pathology can be seen as providing a uniquely formed individual experience and identity. Jung wrote regarding neurosis:

> "We should . . . experience what it means, what it has to teach, what its purpose is. We should even learn to be thankful for it, otherwise . . . [we] miss the opportunity of getting to know ourselves as we really are . . . We do not cure it—it cures us."[8]

Following alchemy, Jung posited a spiritual dynamic of intentionality in psychic change, such that disorder and affliction served as the gateway to achieve psychological wholeness. He expressed in the last interview of his life:

"To this day God is the name by which I designate all things which cross my willful path violently and recklessly, all things which upset my subjective views, plans intentions, to change the course of my life for better or worse."[9]

In other words, "Man needs difficulties."[10] For Jung, gods had "become the diseases,"[11] the symptom is "an attempt at healing,"[12] and "the patient cures the doctor"[13] with the latter "sinking into the emotional disturbance."[14] Suffering the symptom "mothers" the patient as a reenactment of Christ on the Cross.[15] Neurosis, as that which is most antagonistic to the ego, holds "the undeveloped personality, a precious fragment of the psyche."[16] It is the place where the *daimones* of the underworld can make their entrance allowing for a new order, and its emergence signals the transformative process towards the wholeness of the personality. Psychosis, (literally "enlivening the soul") would then be the necessary breakdown for renewed personality to be formed. Depression becomes a mythical event, an enactment of the hero's "night-sea journey," a "dark night of the soul," necessary to attain renewal, and anxiety, the signal of instability, which allows for the possibility of transformation.

In this light, what we call psychopathology is a mythology of our time, the place of the appearance of the gods, a world where desire strives for a place providing a creative, identity-forming ground for the soul, which is inevitably embedded in mythic image. At the same time, the alchemical clinician needs to use method to help the natural process unfold. The word method stems from the Greek word *hodos* or road, and the move is one of opening. Hence, what we see Freud refer to as the building of the ego: the inducement of regression, the teasing out of complexes, the interpretation of defenses are vital as a necessary reductive approach in addressing pathology through "analysis," etymologically, "tearing apart."

Christou focuses on Jung's notion of "symbol" as functioning in the same way as "concept" in philosophy and detached sensible "perception" in science. Jung would say, "The place or the medium of realization is neither mind nor matter, but that intermediate realm of subtle reality which can be adequately expressed only in the symbol."[17] Christou's vision of "observation" ultimately implies a fluidity, a relativity, in that the observed is a function of the language through which it is interpreted and expressed in relation to the personality of the observer as object of experience *to the subject*. The tables are now turned, and observer has become subject to the observed as observed is subject to observer. Here, we have a glimpse of the intersubjectival sensibility of the multilayered field in the psychoanalytic engagement, but also of an animated vision of psychopathology as an encounter with the subjectivity of the "other."

Psychopathology, at its roots, indicates: *psyche*, or "soul," pathos or "experience," "happening," "what befalls," what moves emotionally, especially the feeling of suffering, and finally, *logos* or "word." Psychopathology, then, is the expression given to the experience of the soul's movement, its eventfulness, especially that which involves suffering. In delving into the nature of psychopathology, we are led to a paradoxical sensibility, articulated by James Hillman: pathology is central to psychological life.

Hillman introduces the term:

". . . *pathologizing* to mean the psyche's autonomous ability to create illness, morbidity, disorder, abnormality, and suffering in any aspect of its behavior and to experience and imagine life through this deformed and afflicted perspective."[18]

Pathology as a fundamental ontological strand woven into the complexity of everyday consciousness. The psychological intention of pathology as an agency or ubiquitous, underlying dark force, is one of deconstruction, to open space for a diversification of consciousness away from the comfortable singularity of ego consciousness into a multiplicity of perspectives. "*If the fundamental principle of psychological life is differentiation, then no single perspective can embrace psychological life, and norms are the delusions of that parts prescribe to one another.*"[19]

Psychopathology is the manifestation of the fundamental disordering nature of psyche, a dark upwelling which runs through the ground of universal, cultural and individual attempts to resist it. The history of depth psychology can be seen as the story of attempting to extract meaning from the "other" that presents itself as affliction, to make order of disorder, to find rationality in the irrational, and in a further sense to integrate matter and spirit, body and mind, tangible and transcendent.[20]

Early in his career, Freud saw the "matter" of the psyche in terms of bodily drives, which could be expressed in terms of the transcendent through myth, principally that of Oedipus. He also wrote *The Psychopathology in Everyday Life* in which he presented daily life (mundane) as one fraught with unconscious manifestations (transcendent) resulting in mistakes, slips of the tongue, etc. In his later years, when he had turned to the ego as the center of psychoanalytic focus, his introductory remarks to *The Problem of Anxiety* placed "symptoms" on the same spectrum as "inhibitions." An inhibition is related to a disfunction in the workings of ego, part of which is unconscious, which when taken to an extreme in energy exists beyond ego control becoming a symptom or "morbid process."[21] Freud sets up a structuring of the psyche that presumes a normative mode through a well-structured ego functioning (rational order) via compromise formation between the instinctual needs of the id (matter) and the moral compass of the super ego (transcendent). The ego then becomes prone to infirmity when confronted by the symptom system with enough energy to become free of control by the ego organization (irrational, split off complex) "a thing that is more foreign to the ego than anything else in the mind."[22] It is the symptom, the "other," as independent to ego that is the "starting point"[23] for exploration of the psyche in service to the ego. Freud posits an ordering system (ego) and one of disorder (symptom) that lie upon a continuous spectrum yet are independent of each other. He holds that "order," or ego control, can be reestablished through a process of recognition, adaptation, and assimilation—a rational cause-effect exploration and integration of the disorder on the ego's modified terms which act as "defenses."

For Freud, late in his career, the ego, having a part-location in both id and super ego, carries on a constant struggle to maintain order by avoiding conflict and disturbance from each of the two: order and disorder constantly at odds—the ego caught between the two.

> "The ego is peace-loving and would like to incorporate the symptom, to include it in its ensemble. The *disturbance* proceeds from the symptom . . ." (italics mine)[24]

The prefix "dis" bespeaks the paradoxical nature of the psychological underworld from which the symptom emerges. Originally, Dis was the Roman god of the underworld (Greek, *Hades*), and Dante uses the name as the signifier of the Inferno. Heraclitus refers to him as at one with Dionysus, who reveals himself through dramatic spectacle akin to the "display" (*dis* or apart, *plicare* or fold) of the symptom. On the one hand, "dis" means "utterly," "mostly," "in excess," as in "dis-turb," where turb connotes a *prima materia* of swirling or tumult, *a* surplus of turbulence. Paradoxically, "dis" also means the opposite, "lacking" or "apart from," as in "dis-order." In the syllable "dis" we now have a forerunner to the interactive nature of order and disorder implied by Freud, fullness (order) and emptiness (disorder) rooted at the base.

Ultimately, Freud neared his end with a sobering question: can there be such a thing as a natural end to analysis? His answer was ambivalent—yes, but only to the extent that over a period of time, a patient's defenses can be strengthened and the force of the instincts be diminished such that the two sides are "brought into harmony" with the instincts no longer "seeking for independent satisfaction."[25] However, ultimately the psyche as a whole has it over the ego in that variables are a constant unseen possibility— external conditions that affect the ego's functioning, an energy gain in a new set of instincts, new pathways may open for familiar instincts, previously concealed inherited dispositions in the ego may become revealed, even archetypal factors, "deposits from primitive human development in our archaic heritage"[26] may come into play. In other words, an inherent resistance from the id to be analyzed is always present. "So, not only the patient's analysis but that of the analyst himself has ceased to be a terminable and become an interminable task."[27] An early idea of Freud's indicating the ubiquitous shadow of chaos' reign holds sway even in the end:

" . . . much will be gained if we succeed in transforming . . . hysterical misery into common unhappiness."[28]

Jung subordinates the ego to a greater degree than Freud. Jung used the term in myriad ways, but his consistent and predominant sense is that the ego is one of many parts of the wholeness of personality, the self, and as such is encompassed by and emerging from the latter.

"The ego stands to the self as the moved to the mover or as object to subject, because the determining factors which radiate out from the self-surround the ego on all sides and are therefore supraordinate to it. The self, like the unconscious is an a *priori* existent out of which the ego evolves."[29]

The self is essentially distinct from or a "prefiguration" of the ego, "completely outside the personal sphere."[30] The ego provides a difference of standpoint but ultimately is a:

". . . dark body . . . full of unfathomable obscurities . . . [and] as a *relatively constant personification of the unconscious itself* . . . [becomes] the Schopenhauerian mirror in which the unconscious becomes aware of its own face."[31]

The sense here is that ego is best understood as a given agent, reflecting the luminosities of the unconscious. In Jung's evolved alchemical thinking, the notion of self comes to emphasize the unique particularity of each individual soul where individuation is the "process by which a man becomes the definite unique being he in fact is, to become what he really is,"[32] for "one cannot live from anything except what one is."[33]

192

James Hillman pushes the subjugation of ego to an extreme, insisting that a focus on ego through the ego, such as the notion of ego-self axis produces a narrow horizon to the soul's width and depth and misses the multiplicity that is the make-up of personality with its soulfulness carried by the various subjectivities that make up the whole, which is greater than the sum of its parts. He calls for a view of pathology that acknowledges and entertains the subjectivity of other that is making itself known through pathology and thereby disavows the guiding light of "treatment" as a colonizing of the psyche. Fundamental to this modality is Jung's notion of psyche as exhibited and experienced through image itself as the carrier of meaning.[34] Hillman asks, what does the disease want? Similar to Wittgenstein and Christou's objection to scientific language, he condemns the official, conceptualized, objectifying, rational language, which analysts use to lend themselves authority and validity, as being abstract and reified, separating doctor and patient from a phenomenon that is attempting to join with them in the world of experience. Hillman follows Freud in emphasizing the importance of symptoms, but sees them as the *via extremis—* base, grotesque, putrefying, manic, leaden—through which the soul gains depth and uniqueness of character. Each disorder has its own order, its own way of seeing that which the normative ego can't see, to the phenomenology of the symptom, its archetypal background and intentionality as revealed through lived experience. The wound is the eye; the symptom is the soul.

Hillman is not denying the pain or the working of personal complexes, rather he is transferring the personalizing of the event of psychopathology from the individual to the infirmity. Following alchemical sensibility, the travail is that of the matter being worked upon in the psyche, the wound itself is suffering, baking, decomposing, fragmenting, dissolving, coagulating, stretching, and contracting. It is the ego being shrunk in the hot box, the lead of depression being softened, the fire of Ares burning out in anger, the sulfur of mania spreading, the waters of Heraclean cleansing.

The complex, the historical life reliving itself, is of a separate order from the symptom and from the archetype. The suffering in the complex is not necessarily causal, the past causing the present, rather the life of the complex transcends time, the past events preparing for the present go round, as the present remembers the past. Archetype, complex, symptom—autonomous but related systems—open into each other on a hierarchal structure—the archetypal, background to the complex taking priority in value in its universality, while the complex with its historical life force lies inside the symptom of the moment. Finally, if we extend the idea of the autonomy and inter-relatability of these orders, the symptom, the complex, the archetype, we might imagine each of the three *attracting* the other two: symptom to complex and archetype, complex to symptom and archetype, archetype to symptom and complex.

Nathan Schwartz-Salant[35] wrote on the universal nature of the interaction of systems of order and disorder and, following Jung, starts with the two laws of thermodynamics:
1) conservation of energy: the total amount of energy in any system never changes,
2) entropy: energy in any system is always moving from order to disorder.

The implication here is that any systemic order will always engender an irreversible dynamic toward disorder. Order and disorder are inseparable; there will always be a disorganizing disrupting element in any form of organization. In terms of psychic structure, the ego, seen as ordering factor, uses rational logic, cause-effect reasoning, compromise formation to avoid the pain (anxiety) caused by the intrusion of foreign (unconscious) elements, which, when taken to their extreme are seen as causing pathology (symptom). Furthermore, because the total amount of energy in any system is constant, systems are holographic in nature, that is each part is inter-related containing something of the whole. The inevitable "foreign" (disorder) aspect is always part of the picture, along with the centralized order, "and while any piece of the hologram contains the whole image, it does not hold all the information defining the image. This defect is termed 'noise'. . . . any part we study . . . all the information of the other parts is contained within it . . ."[36] Wherever an order is created, a disorder or "noise" will appear in conjunction, and the analytic event will always be a matter of a field encompassing analyst and patient in multiple systems and rendering ultimate attitudes of certainty or authority on the part of the analyst problematic. The analytic session, like any system, will always be moving toward the emergence of a disorder in the mix.

Schwartz-Salant references mythical reflections of the necessity of disorder. *Ananke* is the Greek primordial goddess of force, constraint, and inevitability, also known as Errant Cause, mother and dictator of the Fates with her spindle. It was said that even the gods would not fight her. For Plato, Necessity as *Ananke*, is the compulsory aspect of life that brings about change through chaos and discord, "the indeterminate, the inconstant, the anomalous, that which can neither be understood, nor predicted."[37] *Khaos* and *Ananke* were at the Beginning:

> ". . . finding the whole visible sphere not at rest but moving in an irregular and disorderly fashion, out of disorder he brought order." (*Timeas*, 30a)[38]

> "Wherefore the mother and receptacle of all created and visible and in any way sensible things . . . is an invisible and formless being which receives all things and in some mysterious way partakes of the intelligible and is most incomprehensible." (*Timeus*, 51a)

Ananke is necessary as a matter of Becoming, which can only occur from disorder to order.

> ". . . the creation of this world is the combined work of necessity and mind. Mind, the ruling power, persuaded necessity to bring the greater part of created things to perfection . . . the variable cause . . . and its influence (must be included)." (*Timeus*, 47e – 48A)

Freud suggests Ananke is necessary for the establishment of civilization itself:

"We can only be satisfied therefore, if we assert that the
process of civilization is modification which the vital
process experiences under the influence of a task that
is set by Eros and instigated by Ananke—by individuals
into a community bound together by libidinal ties."[39]

The art of alchemy asserts in many ways the paradox that
disorder is an achievement in the on-going evolutionary process
of creation of any certain order. Paracelsus asserted, "Destroy
the bodies," and that the entire movement of the project was
from one death to the next. For many alchemists *nigredo* as the
realm of "blacker than black," fragmentation, chaos, putrefaction,
decay and death was a necessary starting position from which
subsequent operations were to proceed. "Inspirit the matter;
materialize the spirit," and "make haste slowly" were paradoxical
prescriptions for action. Operations consisted in grinding up,
burning, dismembering, drowning, and suffocating so that the
experience of torture that comes with change is suffered by the
material (*prima materia*) being worked upon. The "winged" was
paired with the "wingless," the eagle with the toad, and the head
with tail; the work itself is an *opus contra naturum* (contrary
to the natural). The goal is imaged 1) in grotesque figures, 2)
as lying at the base of the Nile to be attained by going *against*
the current and is 3) found in shit. In alchemy, order is always
inviting disorder, and disorder is always a preparation for order,
in a perpetual spiraling movement toward the goal-never-to-be-
attained inherent in an on-going process.

Continuing our dual theme of a predominant dynamic of
the psyche as an interaction between order and disorder and the
nature of psychopathology as the expression of an unrecognized
but inevitable disorder, we now conclude with a meditation on
a particular condition of infirmity, that of the borderline. We
have seen that disorder is not only necessary, but in fact takes
priority over order in the natural world.[40] This idea brings us to
a reimagining of "borderline," conventionally seen as a primary
disease of disorder. Symptomatically, the borderline condition is
marked by a fundamental lack in differentiation of self from other,

personal from environmental, and conscious from unconscious. The individual must gain a sense of self through clinging to an other, using the other to experience feelings, perceptions, and being itself. While the individual, desperately fearful of abandonment and intensely needy of connection, tends to merge with other in order to feel alive, he or she is also paranoically fearful of invasion and devouring, rendering intimacy as a dire threat from which to distance while at the same time yearning for it and venting at its experienced absence. Internal life fluctuates violently between chaos and calm. Intense affect of rage instantly is replaced with seeming contentment. Body is figuratively (and sometimes literally) dismembered and experienced as external objects of which to be jealous. ("My boobs are my only asset!") Reality testing is fraught with unconscious spillover. Poor capacity for object constancy leaves the world either all good/ ideal or all bad/hateful, as is the fragile sense of self. One is under constant scrutiny from the borderline, any indication of difference experienced as hostile aggression worthy of violent retaliation, disparagement and contempt. Any suggestion of misperception or disagreement brings denial, a cloud of gaslighting, and impulsive action bringing chaotic disruption to whatever order has been established in the moment. Love is expressed through destruction, hate, through clinging, void and abyss alternate with a cornucopia of false fullness. Underneath it all, is a volcanic rage ready to erupt without notice, and further down a whirlwind of dread, and at bottom a searing self-loathing.

The dismembering dynamics of the borderline condition are engendered through a severely fragmented infancy and chaotic early childhood environmental atmosphere and ambivalent attitude toward the budding psyche begot by significant others. This presence is void of tolerance for impulses of the infant and child toward destruction and separation, and affects are stonewalled. The psyche is unable to integrate a cohesive sensibility of self, such that experiences of good and bad and affects related to need, fear, rage, guilt, shame, and emptiness as well as feelings of fullness and gratification can be held in a unified self-image.

We now follow Jung and Hillman and ask, who is the god in the infirmity and what does the disease want? If we start with animal nature in the psyche, a totem animal, we come up with coyote, fox and hare, but also an even more primitive creature . . . consider the cockroach. The cockroach lives in a borderline milieu, the crooks and crannies of households, slithering its way through cracks and crevices. It is a night creature, and when visible appears totally disgusting and unnerving, especially when in the form of a swarm as if one impenetrable, heaving, scuttling mass hat can pull one into its mess—the kind of presence one simply doesn't want around. It is highly intelligent and carries a sophisticated warning system making it seemingly impossible: to get rid of—difficult to kill because it can fly, it's body collapses in on itself and it easily generates resistance to repellents. Yet, the retreat of cockroaches brings a profound relief paradoxically giving rise to a new-found sense of what home is (however temporary.) Cockroach species extend back over 300 million years, and have evolved to be able to eat anything, and survive in any environmental condition. As an outsider, the cockroach symbolizes that which undermines ruling order through perseverance while displaying its own unique beauty. At the same time, it is a source of human food and medicine and is essential for natural creation of compost in forests. "The cockroach represents an elemental power *profoundly* archaic, entrenched and adaptable, which slipping through the walls of our defenses, proliferates in the chthonic and the primal, eludes our calculated attempts at repression, and disappearing from one room of our existence, inevitably reappears in another."[41]

We can suggest that the deity of the disorder is itself borderline in many ways, the archetypal Trickster.[42] The Trickster, cross-culturally, is a primitive being, half animal, half god, gender ambivalent. It stands as the antithesis of the cultural hero in that his sense of purpose is one of self-gratification and self-indulgence, in service to his own passions, and it makes its way through guile and deception at others' expense as well as his own. Her actions are impulsive and in service to self-gain, often ending in self-destruction, from which she emerges perpetually anew, but leaving a cultural gift in the process. He crashes into a pile of his own dung and then uses the pile to ascend to a higher level. It is disembodied, detaching and reattaching organs at will, while interchanging gender as convenient, a shapeshifter, instantaneously disappearing and reappearing in multiple forms knowing no boundaries.

Directly and indirectly, the Trickster undermines any aspect of cultural order, whether by tossing the previously ordered stars into the heavens or blowing the earth's people to its four corners with wind from his anus. While he is foolish, Trickster is also a creator god, at once leading the people into higher stages of being and establishing lasting aspects of civilization through his own follies—the presence of ambivalence itself—creator/destroyer, giver/negator, buffoon/benefactor. Her ultimate gift is the persistent reminder: presence merely signifies, stability is always shaky, results will carry unpredictability, reason will be shaken by the logic of irrationality, progress is relativized by regression, disorder will find its way, the rug is ready to be pulled. In other words, what the Trickster/borderline manifests is a certain vitality, albeit self-centered and draining of others, and what it wants is a disavowal of any notion of "reality" as given, an abandonment of received narratives with their expectations and assumptions, and a preparedness to meet the moment on its terms.

Susan Rowland has written on Jung's essay regarding the Trickster, seeing in this archetype a counter to an approach to the psyche based on an orientation around the superiority of ego and its developmental dependence on the linear progression of the hero.[43] In her view, the Trickster is a personification of synchronicity and acausality countering understanding via a patriarchal masculinized objectification of experience through rationality. When depth psychology talks about the psyche as object, it misses the trickster reality that everything is perceived *through* psyche as a process. There is a trickster shadow to every illuminated perception undermining knowledge based on rational orientation. The Trickster draws us into a relationally based feminized knowledge, synchronicity an ever-present phenomenon in creation. Here, Rowland draws attention to the mythic image that it is out of the body of chaos as void that the earth takes its form. Out of lack, meaning emerges.

Following Rowland's sense of the relevance of Trickster for postmodern thinking, what might be gathered of the meaning the trickster/borderline phenomenon brings? First, we note that the political environment of American culture is one of a borderline nature; its splitting, disavowal of inequities and exclusivity, hostile aggression and manipulation all covering underlying cultural fear and despair. Also, noteworthy is that the primary religious strain in the cultural narrative, that of the Bible, originates with a solitary divinity, Jahveh, displaying borderline qualities of relating to his children through alternating rage and seduction while demanding absolute loyalty. We have already seen that a unitary identity is an illusion based on its inter-relational nature and its multiple self-states based on context. Development itself can be seen as evolving through series of self-destructive events, as Winnicott references infants, and deaths as Paracelsus insists in regard to the alchemical process. It follows that the borderline experience helps to diffuse the psyche-suffocating fallacy of linear progression of the hero. The borderline elicits our own rage, despair, emptiness, envy, idealization, and self-doubt. Finally, the borderline/trickster, eluding capture and fixity, undermining closure, brings consciousness down to earth giving a kind of life energy to the situation, forcing an abandonment of dualities, rational assessments, plans, values, interpretations, to exist for the moment, despite ego resistance, sans a rational mode oriented around space and time. Contemporary physics sees the "edge of chaos" in the inter-relationship of natural systems to be the occasion for the emergence of unpredictable change. If we can see that the psyche is borderline, then the only certainty is that the world of chaos will always be lurking around, challenging the received collective narrative, ready to swirl and squirm its way to another awakening of consciousness.

Out of the Work emerges the Mess . . .

Endnotes

[1] Christou falls within the vast framework of phenomenology and linguistics which covers different aspects of the ground he is trying to plow—Husserl's bracketing subjectivity, Dilthey's, Giorgi's, and Devereux's formulations of a human science, Polanyi's sense of scientific knowledge as tacit, Merleau-Ponty's vision of the body as itself ensouled, Lacan's notion of language itself as the fundamental structure of the psyche, Bakhtin's explication of language as carnival playing the subject, and Derrida's notion of the uncertainty of language as trickster/zombie always undermining the promise of "authority."

[2] Jung, C. G., *Psychological Types*, CW 6, pp. 51-2.

[3] *Ibid*, p. 52.

[4] Jung, *Psychology and Alchemy*, CW 12, p. 274 ff.

[5] Jung, "Spirit and Life" in *The Structure and Dynamics of the Psyche*, CW 8, p. 328.

[6] Jung, "On the Nature of the Psyche," p. 204.

[7] Jung, *Mysterium Coniunctionis*, CW 14, p. 180.

[8] Jung, "The State of Psychotherapy Today," in *Civilization in Transition*, CW 10.

[9] Jung, "Why I Believe in God," interview with Kaarle Nordenstreng, *Good Housekeeping*, June, 1961.

[10] Jung, "The Transcendent Function" p. 73.

[11] Jung, *Alchemical Studies*, CW 13, p. 37.

[12] Jung, "The Structure of the Psyche," p. 149.

[13] Jung, *Civilization in Transition*, CW 10.

[14] Jung, "The Transcendent Function," p. 82.

[15] Jung, *Mysterium Coniunctionis*, CW 14, pp. 35-7

[16] Jung, "The State of Psychotherapy Today," in *Civilization in Transition*, CW 10, p. 167.

[17] Jung, *Psychology and Alchemy*, CW 12283

[18] See Hillman, J. (1975) "Pathologizing," in *Re-Visioning Psychology*, p. 57.

[19] *Ibid*, p. 88.

[20] Cultural historical precedents for addressing this tension in one direction or another include the edict of Church Fathers of antiquity proclaiming experience to be founded in either spirit or matter, Kant's discrimination between the knowable (appearance) and the unknowable (essence), and on the other hand, the Romantic revolt against Reason.

[21] Freud, S., *The Problem of Anxiety*, p. 11.

[22] Freud, *Introductory Lectures on Psycho-Analysis*, p. 78.

[23] *Ibid*.

[24] Freud, (1963) 28.

[25] Freud, "Analysis Terminable and Interminable" in *Therapy and Technique*, p. 243.

[26] *Ibid*, p. 259.

[27] *Ibid*, p. 268.

[28] Freud, "The Psychotherapy of Hysteria" in S. Freud and J. Breuer, *Studies in Hysteria*, p. 351.

[29] Jung, "Transformation Symbolism in the Mass" in *Psychology and Religion*, CW 11, p. 259.

[30] Jung, *Aion*, CW 9ii, p. 30.

[31] Jung, *Mysterium Coniunctionis*, CW 14, p. 107.

[32] Jung, "The Relations between the Ego and the Unconscious," in *Two Essays on Analytical Psychology*, CW 7, p. 174.

[33] Jung, *Mysterium Coniunctionis*, CW 14, p. 231.

[34] See Hillman's three essays on image in *Spring 1977, 1978, 1979*.

[35] Schwartz-Salant, N., *The Order-Disorder Paradox*.

[36] *Ibid*, p. 20-21.

[37] *Ibid*, p. 35.

[38] Plato, *Timaeus*, in *The Collected Dialogues of Plato*.

[39] Freud, S. (1961) *Civilization and Its Discontents*, p. 140.

[40] Theories of chaos and complexity in contemporary physics suggest that what we see as predictable order is relevant for only a small portion of natural phenomena.

[41] A. Rosenberg and K. Martin eds., "Cockroach" in *The Book of Symbols*, p. 224.

[42] Jung, "On the Psychology of the Trickster Figure," in *The Archetypes and the Collective Unconscious*, CW 9i, and Radin, P., *The Trickster*.

[43] Rowland, Susan, "Culture, Ethics, and Synchronicity and the Goddess of Synchronicity" in *Jung as a Writer*.

Bibliography

Adler, G. (ed.). (1973). *C.G. Jung Letters*. Vol. 1: 1906-1950. Princeton, NJ: Princeton University Press.

Bergman, R. (1973). "A School for Medicine Men," *American Journal of Psychiatry*, 130:6, June 1973.

Bonus, Petrus of Ferrara. (1974). *The New Pearl of Great Price*. New York: Arno Press.

Buber, M. (1970). *I and Thou*. Translated by Walter Kaufmann. New York: Scribners.

Burckhardt, Titus. (1971). *Alchemy: Science of the Cosmos, Science of the Soul*. Translated from the German by William Stoddart. Baltimore, MD: Penguin Books.

____. (1971). *"Theatrum sapientiae aeternae"* by Heinrich Kunrath.

Dougherty, N. and West, J. (2007). *The Matrix and Meaning of Character*. New York: Routledge.

Edinger, Edward. (1985). *Hermetic Museum*, in *The Anatomy of the Psyche*. LaSalle, IL: Open Court.

____. (1985). *Anatomy of the Psyche: Alchemical Symbolism in Psychotherapy*. La Salle, IL: Open Court Press.

Eliot, T. S. (1952). *The Complete Poems and Plays 1909-1950*. New York: Harcourt World and Brace.

Ellenberger, H. (1970). *The Discovery of the Unconscious*. New York: Basic Books.

Entralgo, P. (1970). *The Therapy of the Word in Classical Antiquity*. Edited and translated by Rather, L. and Sharp, J. New Haven, CT: Yale University Press.

Esslin, M. (1961). *The Theatre of the Absurd*. New York: Doubleday.

Euripides. (1963). "Medea" in *Medea and Other Plays*. Translated and Introduction by Philip Wellscott. London: Penguin.

Freud, S. (1912). "Recommendations to Physicians Practicing Psycho-analysis" in *Standard Edition*. London: Imago Publishing.

_____. (1933) *Introductory Lectures on Psycho-Analysis*. Translated by W. J. H. Sprott. London: Hogarth.

_____. (1961) *Civilization and Its Discontents*, Translated by James Strachey, New York: Norton.

_____. (1963) *The Problem of Anxiety*. Translated by Henry Bunker. New York: Norton.

_____. (1966). *Studies in Hysteria*. New York: Avon.

Gill, S. (1977). "Prayer As Person: The Performative Force in Navajo Prayer Acts," *History of Religions*, 17:2, August, 1977.

Groesbeck, J. (1975). "The archetypal image of the wounded healer," Vol 20. No. 2, *The Journal of Analytical Psychology*.

Hartigan K. (2009). *Performance and Cure: Drama and Healing in in Ancient Greece and Contemporary America*. London: Duckworth.

Hillman, J. (1975). *Re- Visioning Psychology*. New York: Harper and Row.

_____. (1979). *The Dream and the Underworld*. New York: Harper and Row.

_____. *Spring*, 1977, 1978, 1979. Dallas, TX: Spring Publications.

Holy Bible (New Revised Standard Version). (1989). Oxford: Oxford University Press.

Homer. (1967). *The Odyssey of Homer*. Translated with an introduction by R. Lattimore. New York: Harper and Row.

Homer. (1951). *The Iliad of Homer*. Translated with an Introduction by R. Lattimore. Chicago: The University of Chicago Press.

Jung C. G. (1951). *Aion, Collected Works*, vol. 9ii. Translated by R.F.C. Hull. Princeton, NJ: Princeton University Press.

_____. (1953). *Psychology and Alchemy, Collected Works*, vol. 12. Translated by R.F.C. Hull. Princeton, NJ: Princeton University Press.

_____. (1953). "The Relations between the Ego and the Unconscious," in Two *Essays on Analytical Psychology*,

Collected Works, vol. 7. Translated by R.F.C. Hull. Princeton, NJ: Princeton University Press.

_____. (1954). *The Practice of Psychotherapy, Collected Works*, vol. 16. Translated by R.F.C. Hull. Princeton: Princeton University Press.

_____. (1958). *Psychology and Religion: West and East, Collected Works*, vol. 11. Translated by R.F.C. Hull. Princeton: Princeton University Press.

_____. (1959). "On the Psychology of the Trickster Figure," in *The Archetypes and the Collective Unconscious, Collected Works*, vol. 9i. Translated by R.F.C. Hull. Princeton, NJ: Princeton University Press.

_____. (1960). *The Structure and Dynamics of the Psyche, Collected Works*, vol. 8. Translated by R.F.C. Hull. Princeton, NJ: Princeton University Press.

_____. (1961). *Memories, Dreams, Reflections*. Recorded and Edited by Aniela Jaffé. Translated by Richard and Clara Winston. New York: Random House.

_____. (1961) "Why I Believe in God," interview with Kaarle Nordenstreng, *Good Housekeeping*, June, 1961.

_____. (1963). *Mysterium Coniunctionis, Collected Works*, vol. 14. Translated by R.F.C. Hull. Princeton, NJ: Princeton University Press.

_____. (1964a). *Civilization in Transition, Collected Works*, vol. 10. Princeton, NJ: Princeton University Press.

_____. (1967). *Alchemical Studies, Collected Works*, vol. 13. Translated by R.F.C. Hull. Princeton: Princeton University Press.

_____. (1971). *Psychological Types, Collected Works*, vol. 6. Translated by R.F.C. Hull. Princeton, NJ: Princeton University Press.

Kerenyi, K. (1959). Asklepios: *Archetypal Image of the Physician's Existence*. New York: Pantheon Books.

_____. (1967). *Eleusis: Archetypal Image of Mother and Daughter*. Translated by Ralph Manheim, Princeton, NJ: Princeton University Press.

Kugler, P. (2002). *The Alchemy of Discourse: Image, Sound and Psyche*. Eisiedeln: Daimon Verlag.

Lacan, J. (1949). "The mirror stage as formative of the function of the I as revealed in psychoanalytic experience" in *Escrits*. New York: W. W. Norton.

_____. (1977). "Seminar on the 'Purloined Letter'" in *Escrit: A Selection*. Translated by Alan Sheridan, New York: W. W. Norton.

Lindner, R. (1955). *The Fifty-Minute Hour*. New York: Bantam.

Meier, C. (1967). *Ancient Incubation and Modern Psychotherapy*. Translated by Monica Curtis. Evanston, IL: Northwestern University Press.

Melchior-Bonnet, S. (2001). *The Mirror: A History*. Translated by Katherine H. Jewett with a preface by Jean Delumeau. New York: Routledge.

Merleau-Ponty, M. (1964). "The Child's Relation to Others" in *The Primacy of Perception*. Evanston, IL: Northwestern University Press.

Muller, J. P., and Richardson, W. J. (Eds.). (1988). *The Purloined Poe*. New York: Putnam.

Ogden, T. (1994). *Subjects of Analysis*, NJ: Jason Aronson.

Plato. (1961). *The Collected Dialogues of Plato*. Edited by Hamilton, E. and Cairns, H. "Phaedrus." Translated by R. Hackforth. Princeton, NJ: Princeton University Press.

Radin, P. (1959). *The Trickster*. New York: Schocken Press.

Reichard, G. (1963). *Navaho Religion: A Study of Symbolism*. Princeton, NJ: Princeton University Press.

Ronnberg, A. and Martin, K. (eds.). *The Book of Symbols*. Koln: Taschen.

Rowland, S. (2005). *Jung as a Writer*. New York: Routledge.

Sandner, D. (1979). *Navaho Symbols of Healing*. New York: Harcourt Brace Jovanovich.

Sartre, J. P. (1953). *Being and Nothingness: an Essay on Phenomenological Ontology*. Translated with an Introduction by Hazel E. Barnes. New York: Washington Square Press.

Schwartz-Salant, N. (1989). *The Borderline Personality: Vision and Healing*, Wilmette, IL: Chiron Publications.

_____. (2017). *The Order-Disorder Paradox*, Berkeley, CA: North Atlantic.

Sedgwick, D. (1994). *The Wounded Healer*, New York: Routledge.

Stavenhagen, L. (ed.). (1974). A *Testament of Alchemy*. Hanover, NH: The University Press of New England.

Suzuki, S. (1973). *Zen Mind, Beginners Mind*. New York: Weatherhill.

Turner, V. (1967). *The Forest of Symbols: Aspects of Ndembu Ritual*. Ithaca, NY: Cornell University Press.

_____. (1969). *The Ritual Process*. Ithaca, NY: Cornell University Press.

von Franz, M. L. (1980). *Alchemy: An Introduction to the Symbolism and Psychology*. Toronto: Inner City Books.

Waite, A. (ed.). (1967). *The Hermetic and Alchemical Writings of Aureolus Philippus Theophrastus Bombast of Hohenheim, called Paracelsus the Great*, Vol. II. New Hyde Park, NY: University Books.

_____. (1976). *The Hermetic and Alchemical Writings of Aureolus Philippus Theophrastus Bombast of Hohenheim, called Paracelsus the Great*, Vol. I, Berkeley, CA: Shambhala.

Winnicott, D. W. (1967). "Mirror Role of Mother and Family in Child Development" in *Playing and Reality*. New York: Tavistock.

Witherspoon, G. (1977). *Language and Art in the Navajo Universe*. Ann Arbor, MI: University of Michigan Press.

Index

Name

Subject